Wild Flowers in the Carolinas

Wild Flowers
IN THE CAROLINAS

By Wade T. Batson

University of South Carolina Press

Copyright © University of South Carolina 1987

Published in Columbia, South Carolina, by the
University of South Carolina Press

Second Printing, 1990

Printed in Hong Kong by Everbest Printing Co. Ltd.
Through Four Colour Imports, Ltd., Louisville, KY.

Library of Congress Cataloging-in-Publication Data

Batson, Wade T.
  Wild flowers in the Carolinas

  Includes index.
    1. Wild flowers—North Carolina—Identification
  2. Wild flowers—South Carolina—Identification
  I. Title.
  QK178.B38   1987   582.13'09756   86-30785
  ISBN 0-87249-504-3
  ISBN 0-87249-505-1 (pbk.)

Contents

Introduction

The southeastern states, and particularly the Carolinas, have long been noted for the number, diversity, and development of species of indigenous plants. To this native flora add the cultivars that have been brought here and have escaped cultivation and become established—naturalized—as have Japanese Honeysuckle, Privet, Day Lily, etc., and also those that have come uninvited—introduced unintentionally—as have Crab Grass, Sheep Sorrel, Carpetweed, etc., the total number of species in our "wild" flora well exceeds three thousand. Furthermore, greatly increased world-wide travel and commerce result in a constantly increasing number of introductions some of which find climate and habitat favorable and become established.

Plant distribution within a particular habitat type is controlled by several different factors. For example, rich mountain coves may be found from New York to Georgia but *Shortia*, limited to such sites, is found only in a few small areas in the western Carolinas, and very sparsely there. Some of the more important controlling environmental factors are elevation, the amount and seasonal distribution of rainfall, soil type, acidity and exposure of the site to sunlight, where the amount of cover and the direction of slope are significant.

In their distribution some species are bound together by very specific environmental requirements and for this reason may be thought of as associated species. To those familiar with such associations the presence in an area of one kind of wild plant may indicate the possible or likely occurrence nearby of certain other kinds. The actual discovery of a plant, however, may depend on more than the mere knowledge of the environmental factors controlling its distribution or the species with which it is likely to be associated. Some kinds of plants make their appearance only as spring annuals and are gone by the time summer arrives. Such herbaceous perennials as Trilliums, Violets, and Asters survive the winters by their underground parts only. Woody varieties that seasonally lose their leaves and are known as deciduous are generally more easily recognized when leaves and either flowers or fruits are present. Evergreens are more conspicuous during the winter when other perennials have lost their leaves, and, since there are relatively few kinds of evergreens, identification on the basis of leaf characteristics alone, or leaf characteristics together with growth habit, bark, habitat, etc., is usually not difficult. In some cases fruits or fruit parts persist well into or throughout the winter and may be used in identification.

Nowadays, many of the natural habitats for wildlife are being destroyed by such factors as sprawling urbanization, new and expanding industrial and defense establishments, airport construction, dams, transmission lines and enlargement of state and interstate highway systems, all of which follow the increasing space demands of a rapidly growing population. The once common small fields and pastures separated by woods or hedgerows have now often become extensive developments suited to the mechanized practices of modern agriculture. The sanctuary provided plants and animals by the once intervening woods and hedgerows is now largely gone.

Furthermore, vast acreages throughout the whole southeast have been given over exclusively to the growing of pine trees. A pine plantation of from about 15 to 30 or more years of age is a veritable biological desert. This is due to the fact that the dense canopy and highly competitive root systems of the close-growing pines exclude most other forms of plant life during this period, and since the pines offer little in the way of either food or shelter for animal life, few kinds are found there. In a closed stand of this kind, however, there is little or no pine reproduction and if left undisturbed, which is not usually the case, the pines would eventually be replaced by the more photosynthetically efficient broad-leafed plants. This would be accomplished through the normal processes of seed dispersal, assuming the existence of adjacent seed sources.

Once a species has been eliminated from some place by destruction of its habitat, the habitat must be reestablished and a seed source conveniently available before the species can recur. Suitable refuge is afforded many marsh-loving species along the shallow margins of ponds and lakes. Highway rights-of-way, despite frequent mowings, serve as refuge for many type of herbaceous plants. And the shift of the population from farms to cities has resulted in the abandonment of many farms, and refuges are reestablished in these situations.

Lately, considerable interest has arisen in the establishment of garden sanctuaries. Often wild plants can be rescued from areas threatened with destruction and moved to some protected location that fairly well matches the original habitat. Many endangered or otherwise noteworthy species are available for acquisition through recognized dealers in wild plants from their nursery propagated stock. Home or public landscaping with such plants is real conservation and such use might afford a last refuge for an increasing number of endangered species. The now widespread Ginkgo tree is said to have been preserved in the monastery gardens of China for so long that its former occurrence and distribution in the Chinese flora is unknown. In a new location, conservation of the plant is successful only when some form of reproduction provides new individuals for the continuation of the species.

Various local, state and federal regulations have been enacted for the protection of wildlife, a term which until quite recently applied only to game animals, game birds and game fishes. In most cases now nongame species and plants are included with emphasis on endangered species and habitat types. Herbarium records indicate that perhaps as many as ten percent of our native plants are presently endangered. This is due largely, if not entirely, to habitat destruction.

In most cases, the species presented here are known to the extent that one or more common names have been given them. The common name along with the scientific name is given. The latter consists of a binomial followed by the name of the person who is the authority for the use of the scientific name. The scientific name is made up of the generic and specific names, both being Latin or Latinized words. The authority represents the person or persons who originally named and published a description of the plant, for example, the scientific name of White Oak is *Quercus alba* Linnaeus. This means that *Quercus*, the genus or generic name, is the name for Oak and is applied to all Oaks. The second part of the binomial, *alba*, is the specific name or species, and indicates the particular kind of Oak, here White Oak. Linnaeus is shown as the authority because he assigned the name *Quercus alba* to this plant and was first to publish an account of it.

In some cases the original author may have placed the plant in a different genus from the one shown. In those cases someone later has decided that the plant should not have been placed in that genus and has moved it to another. Such changes are provided for in International Rules for Botanical Nomenclature. For an example, consider the case of a small red morning glory. It was first described in a publication by Linnaeus as *Ipomoea coccinea*, so it became known as *Ipomoea coccinea* Linnaeus. Later a botanist by the name of Conrad Moench decided that it was enough different from other morning

glories to merit a new or different genus and moved it from *Ipomoea* to the new genus *Quamoclit*. The specific name first assigned always holds, in this case *coccinea*, and the authority for it is always shown but in parentheses, the new name thus becomes *Quamoclit coccines* (Linnaeus) Moench.

Acknowledgment

Grateful acknowledgment is made to the Columbia Garden Club and the Garden Club of South Carolina for their support of this publication.

Glossary

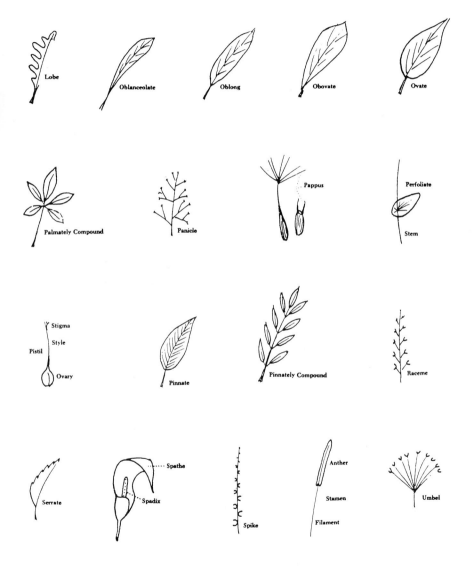

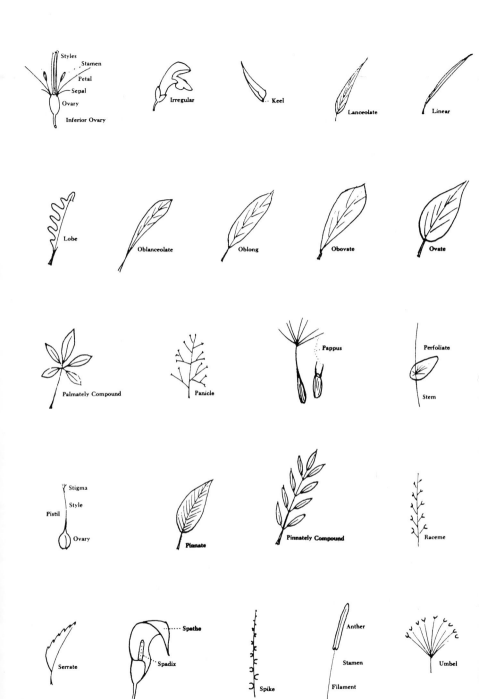

Styles
Stamen
Petal
Sepal
Ovary
Inferior Ovary

Irregular

Keel

Lanceolate

Linear

Lobe

Oblanceolate

Oblong

Obovate

Ovate

Palmately Compound

Panicle

Pappus

Perfoliate

Stem

Stigma
Style
Pistil
Ovary

Pinnate

Pinnately Compound

Raceme

Serrate

Spathe

Spadix

Spike

Anther

Stamen

Filament

Umbel

Abortive—Imperfectly formed.

Acaulescent—Stemless or apparently so.

Achene—A small, dry, indehiscent 1-seeded fruit, as the individual fruits on a strawberry.

Acuminate—Gradually tapering to a slender point.

Acute—Ending in a well-defined angle.

Alternate—Said of parts that are borne singly at different levels on the axis, or situated between other parts.

Ament—A dry scaly spike usually staminate (oaks, hickories).

Annual—Of only one season's duration.

Anther—The pollen-bearing part of a stamen. (**See** stamen)

Attenuate—Tapering so as to become very narrow, said of leaf bases and apices.

Awn—A coarse bristle-like extension. (**See** barb)

Axil—The angle formed between the upper side of the petiole and the stem.

Axillary—Located in an axil, as a bud or flower.

Axis—The main stem or line of development.

Barb—A rigid point inclined upward or downward, usually downward.

Beak—A long prominent point, said of fruits and perigynia.

Berry—A pulpy indehiscent fruit with immersed seeds (tomato, grape).

Biennial—Maturing from seed in two seasons.

Blade—The flat, expanded portion of a leaf.

Bract—A much reduced and sometimes otherwise modified leaf subtending a flower, flower cluster or head.

Bud—An unopened flower or an undeveloped leaf branch usually protected by a covering of scale-like structures.

Bulb—An enlarged vertical underground shoot consisting mainly of fleshy leaf bases (onion, lily).

Calyx—The outer whorl of floral parts made up of individual members known as sepals.

Capillary—Hair-like.

Capsule—A non-fleshy dehiscent fruit made up of two or more carpels.

Carpel—A simple pistil or the unit of structure of a compound pistil.

Chaff—A small, dry, membranous scale or bract found growing on the receptacle subtending the individual flowers in some composites (sunflower).

Ciliate—Fringed with hairs or hair-like divisions.

Claw—The narrowed and elongated base of certain sepals and petals.

Cleistogamous—Applied to small, closed, self-fertilized flowers that are mostly underground (certain violets).

Clone—The group of individuals resulting from the vegetative multiplication of a single plant.

Composite—Compound. A member of the family **Compositae.**

Cordate—Heart-shaped.

Corm—The solid, bulb-like, fleshy base of a stem.

Corolla—The inner floral envelope or series of perianth parts which, separate or united, are known individually as petals.

Crest—A conspicuous ridge or elevation on the surface of an organ.

Cyme—A more-or-less flat-topped flower cluster, the central flowers blooming earliest.

Deciduous—Not evergreen.

Dehiscent—Said of a capsule or stamen with the potential for opening or splitting to discharge its contents.

Dentate—With teeth projecting at right angles, as long margin of leaf.

Diffuse—Loosely spreading.

Dimorphous—Possessing two characteristic shapes or forms, as leaves from high and low branches of some oaks.

Disc flower—In many composites, dimorphism exists with respect to the flowers. Those in the center of the head are referred to as disc or tubular and those on the periphery as ray or ligulate.

Drupe—A fleshy fruit with a hard or stony inner portion (cherry, peach).

Entire—Having the margin continuous and unbroken by teeth, lobes or divisions.

Ephemeral—Persisting for only a day or less.

Epiphyte—A plant growing upon or attached to another plant but deriving no sustenance therefrom; an air plant.

Fertile—Said of a flower capable of producing seeds.

Filament—The part of a stamen that supports the anther. (**See** stamen.)

Floral envelope—The calyx and corolla; the perianth.

Floret—A very small flower, as in grasses.

Fruit—A ripened ovary and its contents; the seed bearing portion of a plant.

Genus—A group of related species, for example the genus **Quercus** contains all species of oaks.

Glabrous—Smooth; without hairs.

Glaucous—Covered or whitened with fine waxy scales, as the surface of many leaves or grapes.

Head—A dense cluster of sessile or nearly sessile flowers usually on a short broad axis or receptacle which is surrounded by bracts called involucral bracts (dandelion).

Herb—A plant having no persistent woody stem above the ground.

Herbaceous—With the characteristics of an herb.

Imperfect—Flowers lacking either stamens or pistil.

Inferior ovary—An ovary which at least in part is grown to or fused with the calyx.

Inflorescence—The arrangement of flowers borne by a plant.

Involucre—A whorl of bracts subtending a flower or flower cluster (dandelion, white-bracted sedge).

Irregular—Members unalike in size and form, as the corollas in the Mint family.

Joint—Node or point of articulation.

Keel—Any structure or structures so folded as to be shaped like the bottom of a boat, as the lower two petals of flowers in the Pea family.

Labiate—Having a corolla made up of united petals but divided into two parts, one projecting over the other so as to present the lipped appearance characteristic of several families particularly the mint.

Lanceolate—Longer than broad and broadest toward the base.

Leaflet—A division of a compound leaf.

Linear—Long and narrow with parallel sides.

Lobe—Segment of an organ, particularly a leaf.

Membranous—Thin and translucent.

Nerve—See vein.

Node—The point on a stem at which leaves are borne.

Oblanceolate—Lanceolate but broadest toward the apex.

Oblong—Longer than broad with parallel sides.

Obovate—Reverse ovate.

Opposite—Applied when two leaves are borne at one node, but so arranged as to be on opposite sides of the stem.

Ovary—The enlarged portion of the pistil. (See pistil).

Ovate—Egg-shaped in outline with the broader end toward the base.

Ovule—A structure in the ovary which develops into a seed.

Palmate—Said of lobes or veins that radiate from a common point (sweet gum leaf).

Palmately compound—Leaf with radiate arrangement of leaflets.

Panicle—An open irregularly branched flower cluster.

Pappus—The modified calyx in members of the composite family. Modification may consist of capillary hairs, bristles, awns, teeth or crown (dandelion).

Parasite—Plant that derives its sustenance from another living plant (dodder).

Pedicel—Stalk of a single flower.

Peduncle—Stalk of a flower cluster or inflorescence.

Perfect—A flower with both stamens and pistil.

Perfoliate—Said of a leaf which gives the appearance of having been pierced by the stem.

Perianth—Floral envelope consisting of both calyx and corolla.

Persistent—Remaining attached after the growing period.

Petal—Division of the corolla. May be separated or attached to others of the series.

Petiole—Stalk-like support of a leaf. (**See** blade)

Pinnate—Said of lobes or veins that form a rather equal pattern along either side of the mid-vein; feather-like.

Pinnately compound—Said of leaves with an arrangement of leaflets along either side of the main axis (sumac).

Pistil—The central structure of the flower; the seed bearing organ.

Pistillate—Having a pistil or pistils, but usually no stamens.

Pollen—Grains or bodies produced by the anther and containing the male element.

Pubescent—Covered with soft usually short hairs.

Raceme—An arrangement of pedicellate flowers borne along an elongated axis.

Ray—See disc.

Receptacle—The expanded end of a flower stalk. (**See** disc)

Regular—Having the members alike in size and form.

Rhizome—Subterranean stem.

Rootstock—Rhizome; a subterranean stem or part of one.

Rosette—A cluster of radiating leaves usually at ground level.

Runner—A slender horizontal branch rooting at the nodes.

Sagittate—Arrow-shaped.

Saprophyte—A plant which utilizes dead organic matter (mushroom).

Sepal—Division of the calyx, either separate from or united with others of the series.

Serrate—With sharp teeth angled forward; sawtoothed.

Sessile—Attached directly without petiole or peduncle.

Shrub—A woody perennial up to several feet in height and usually with several stems.

Sinus—The cleft or space between two lobes.

Spadix—A fleshy spike.

Spathe—The sheathing bract around a spadix.

Spike—An arrangement of sessile flowers on an elongated axis.

Spur—A tubular extension of a corolla.

Stamen—Pollen bearing organ made up of anther and filament.

Staminate—Having stamens but usually no pistil.

Standard—Broad upper petal of the corolla in the Pea family.

Sterile—Said of a flower incapable of producing seeds.

Stipule—One of a pair of leaf-like appendages at the base of a petiole (rose, young leaves of tulip poplar).

Stolon—Runner.

Style—When present a neck-like structure connecting the stigma and the ovary.

Tendril—A slender coiling organ functioning in support.

Tuber—A thick short underground stem (Irish potato).

Tuft—Small stems arising close together; a cluster.

Umbel—An inflorescence in which the stalks supporting the flowers or flower cluster arise from a common point, as the ribs of an umbrella. Umbels are characteristic of the Carrot family.

Vein—A vascular bundle in a leaf or flower part.

Whorl—Three or more leaves or other structures in a circle around a node.

Wing—A membranous extension of an organ, as in fruit of maple or elm.

Flower Parts

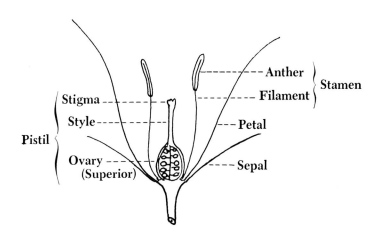

Stamen
— Anther
— Filament

Pistil
{
Stigma
Style
Ovary
(Superior)
}

— Petal

— Sepal

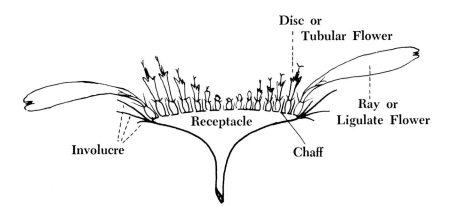

Disc or
Tubular Flower

Ray or
Ligulate Flower

Receptacle

Involucre

Chaff

BUR REED: *Sparganium americanum* Nuttall.

Marsh or aquatic herbs with stout stems up to 4 ft. tall from perennial rhizomes. Leaves thin and sometimes equaling height of plant. Inflorescence simple or branched. Flowers unisexual and in spherical heads. Pistillate below, becoming 1 in. in diameter; staminate above, smaller. Petals none. Margins of swamps, ponds and streams. Summer. Newfoundland to Florida.

The vegetative phase often submerged has long flexuous leaves streaming in the water or floating. Some species of *Scirpus* when under water assume this habit but have leaves only about ¼ in wide.

CATTAIL: *Typha latifolia* Linnaeus.

Erect aquatic herb up to 7 ft. tall. Stem arising from colony-forming perennial rhizomes remarkable for the amount of air space they contain. Leaves glabrous, long-linear and sheathing at the base. Flowers unisexual, minute, densely crowded in cylindric terminal spikes, staminate above, pistillate below. Perianth none. Each tiny flower surrounded by several long silky hairs. Fruit a minute, fusiform achene adapted for dispersal by air currents.

Stream and lake margins and swampy ground. Summer. North America.

T. angustifolia Linnaeus is a somewhat more slender plant usually with staminate and pistillate portions of the spike separated by a distance of ½ in. or more. Occurs mainly along and near the coast.

1

ARROWHEAD: *Sagittaria falcata* Pursh.

Erect, rather coarse aquatic from a large underground starchy stem. Leaves with blades up to 1 ft. long, narrowly elliptic, without basal lobes and with petioles longer than the blades. The inflorescence consists of a leafless stalk to 5 ft. high bearing whorls of flowers or flowering branches. Flowers fragile, 1 in. or more across, made up of 3 inconspicuous green sepals and 3 large white petals. Flowers on the lower part of the inflorescence bear only numerous pistils while those on the upper part may be staminate or mixed.

Swamps, ponds and shallow streams of the lower Coastal Plain. Spring. Delaware to Florida.

SWAMP POTATO, WAMPEE: *S. latifolia* Willdenow.

An erect aquatic herb with broad pointed leaves with conspicuous basal lobes. Flowering stem to 4 ft. tall. Tuberlike rhizomes have high starch content and have been used as food.

Swamps, ponds and shallow streams. Spring. Nova Scotia to Florida, more common inland.

Several other species may be found in the area.

Alisma subcordatum Rafinesque and *Echinodorus cordifolius* (Linnaeus) Grisebach. Similar plants, both with broad leaves and conspicuous cross veins between the main veins. The former is restricted to the Piedmont; the latter to the Coastal Plain.

GIANT REED: *Arundo donax* Linnaeus.

This member of the grass family arises from horizontal rootstocks and attains a height of 6–20 ft. Although somewhat woody, the above ground portion dies each year. It has been introduced into this country from subtropical areas of the Old World and is frequently planted for its bold habit and showy panicles. Variations exist wherein the leaves are striped with either white or yellow.

Widely planted, occasionally escaping cultivation. Late summer. Mediterranean region.

PAMPAS GRASS, *Cortaderia selloana* Aschers and Graebner.

Clump former with large silky panicles raised well above the long basal leaves. Argentina.

Miscanthus sinensis Andersson. Clump former with few-branched, open panicles. Stems leafy on basal half. Leaves green or striped or banded with white. Spreads by seeds. China and Japan.

Phragmites communis Trinius. Tall, leafy-stemmed and with dark panicles, of marshes and wet margins. More common northward.

Oplismenus setarius (Lamarck) Roemer and Schultes. A prostrate and creeping, much-branched, shade-loving, mostly evergreen perennial with stems to 15 in. long and lanceolate to ovate leaves with curiously wavey surfaces; fruiting stems ascending; spikelets long awned. Formerly used in hanging baskets and for borders. Shady margins and low woods, mostly Coastal Plain. Fall. North Carolina and south.

CANE: *Arundinaria gigantea* (Walter) Chapman.

Our only woody grass, semievergreen, forming colonies, or "canebrakes," from rhizomes. Stems are hollow, jointed and branched above. Leaves alternate, lanceolate and to 8 in. long. Flowers are seldom produced. Unless in low, rich, open ground (mostly along streams), stems attain heights of only a few feet.

Found in many different habitats, throughout. Spring. Virginia to Florida and west.

PLUMEGRASS, BEARDGRASS: *Erianthus contortus* Elliott.

Coarse reedlike grass arising from a perennial knotty rootstock. Flowering stems to 7 ft. tall. Blades about ½ in. wide and rough. Inflorescence a tawny-colored, silky panicle. Panicle branches ascending but not closely appressed. Spikelets brownish with a conspicuous terminal awn, which becomes twisted or untwisted in response to changes in humidity; surrounded by long hairs arising from the base.

Moist pinelands and open ground mostly on the Coastal Plain. Late summer and fall. Maryland to Florida.

Other species include *E. strictus* Baldwin and *E. giganteus* (Walter) Muhlenberg. The former has a smaller, scarcely plumey-looking panicle, with closely appressed branches. The latter is more robust with a larger silky panicle.

BROOM SEDGE: *Andropogon virginicus* Michaux.

Perhaps 6 of these perennial grasses adorn the autumn landscape. This common species, in the right foreground, being lithe and leafy was formerly widely used for homemade brooms. The racemes of silky flowers and fruits are largely hidden by sheathing bracts. In the center is *A. glomeratus* (Walter) Britton, Sterns and Pogenbrug in which the inflorescence is compact and glomerately branched. To the left is *A. ternarius* Michaux with racemes exerted well beyond the sheathing bracts; the entire plant is often suffused with purple.

Old fields, open woods, margins and ditch banks. Fall. Delaware to Florida and westward.

4

WHITE-TOP SEDGE: *Dichromena colorata* (Linnaeus) Hitchcock.

Plants to 2 ft. high consisting of perennial rhizomes giving rise to obtusely 3-angled flowering stalks that are leafy at the base. Leaves are narrow and grasslike. The inflorescence is a compact arrangement of sessile spikelets closely subtended by several white or whitish leaflike bracts. The achenes are small and ovoid.

Open wet places mostly in the Coastal Plain. Summer. Virginia to Florida.

DWARF PALMETTO: *Sabal minor* Persoon.

Low palm usually from underground stem but sometimes with short trunk. Leaves 2–4 ft. broad and nearly flat or fan-shaped except for the long segments around the margin; petiole edges lacking teeth. Flowers small, greenish; fruit shining black, globular, ⅓ in. thick. A hardy palm, suitable for cultivation.

Low lands. North Carolina to Florida.

PALMETTO: *S. palmetto* Loddiges.

Native to the coastal area from North Carolina to Florida. State tree of South Carolina and Florida.

SAW PALMETTO: *Serenoa repens* (Bartram) Small.

Seldom over 3 ft. high, rather yellow-green, clump-forming evergreen shrub with very sharp spines along the petioles, found in sandy coastal woods and margins from southern South Carolina south.

Sabal minor

5

JACK-IN-THE-PULPIT, INDIAN TURNIP: *Arisaema triphyllum* (Linnaeus) Schott.

Plant to 2 ft. tall arising from enlarged and horizontally flattened bulbous base. The stalk bears at its summit 2 trifoliate leaves; the leaflets have smooth margins and are gray-green beneath. The individual flowers are small, without much color, without noticeable sepals or petals and are borne on a fleshy spike, or spadix, which extends upward from the axis of the 2 leaves as a club-shaped "jack." This "jack" is very loosely surrounded by a brown striped leaflike bract (the spathe) which toward the tip arches over the "jack" forming the "pulpit." Fruits develop from the lower flowers as a cluster of persistent red berries.

This can be easily grown in a moist, shady place.

Rich, moist woods from the mountains to the coast. Spring. Eastern United States.

DRAGON-ROOT, GREEN DRAGON: *A. dracontium* (Linnaeus) Schott.

Similar to preceding but with only a single leaf with 7–13 long-pointed leaflets and a very long-pointed spathe, the "dragon's tail."

Swamps and damp woods, Piedmont and Coastal Plain. Early summer. Widely distributed in eastern North America.

ARROW ARUM: *Peltandra virginica* (Linnaeus) Kunth.

Perennial from short, stout rootstock; leaves arrow shaped, with 3 main nerves, paler beneath, to 12 in. long and on long leaf stalk. Flowers small and on erect, long-stemmed fleshy spike which is closely surrounded by a fleshy green bract; maturity results in green, 3-seeded berries on a prostrate flower stalk, sometimes under water.

Swamps and wet places, throughout. Spring. Maine to Florida.

GOLDEN CLUB: *Orontium aquaticum* Linnaeus.

Aquatic perennial herb with rhizomes deeply rooted in the mud. Leaves bluish green, oblong, long petioled and usually floating, water repelling and therefore never appearing wet. Flowers yellow, arranged in a fleshy more-or-less club-shaped spike terminating a white stalk later becoming green. Sepals and petals scalelike and inconspicuous. Stamens 4 in the upper flowers, 6 in the lower.

Shallow ponds, stream margins, ditches, and swamps, mostly in the Coastal Plain. Spring. Massachusetts to Florida.

Limnobium spongia (Bosc) Steudel. Shares similar habitats to preceding. From a root system, usually in the mud, a rosette of roundly heart-shaped, long-stalked leaves, thickened underneath by a layer of spongy tissue, and usually a solitary, 3-parted flower arise.

Swamps and marshes, lower Coastal Plain. Summer, Virginia south.

SPIDERWORT: *Tradescantia ohioensis* Rafinesque.

Stems erect, glaucous, up to 2 ft. high from thickened perennial roots. Leaves linear, somewhat keeled and to 1 ft. long. Flowers in clusters from the axis of leaflike bracts, to 1¼ in. across, various shades of purple or rarely white. Petals 3, similar. Fruit a 2- to 3-celled capsule. A satisfactory transplant because of its showy flowers and long blooming season.

Thickets and roadsides. Late spring to summer. Massachusetts to Florida.

SPIDERWORT: *Tradescantia rosea* Ventenat.

Upright herbaceous perennial growing in tufts, stems to 1 ft. tall. Roots, stem and leaves fleshy and juicy. Leaves erect, narrow and less than ¼ in. wide. Sepals 3, short, greenish and pubescent. Petals 3, equal, bright pink or rose and about ½ in. long.

Dry or moist sandy soil in open woods or pinelands. Lower Piedmont and Coastal Plain. Late spring. Virginia to Florida.

DAYFLOWER: *Commelina communis* Linnaeus. Prostrate or ascending glabrous annual with narrowly ovate entire leaves and flowers emerging, one at a time, from a folded bract. After pollination the developing seedpod is drawn back into the bract. Petals 3, 2 conspicious blue ones, 1 small and inconspicuous white.

Common throughout. Summer. Massachusetts south. Asian.

PIPEWORT: *Eriocaulon decangulare* Linnaeus.

Stemless aquatic or marsh plant from a tuft of fibrous roots. Leaves translucent and with obvious cross veins, from 3–10 in. long forming a loose rosette and often under water except during dry periods. Flower stalk to 2 ft. high. Flowers white, very small, irregular in shape and borne in a dense flattened head at the top of a 10-ribbed flower stalk.

Swamps and wet pine woods on the Coastal Plain. Early summer. New Jersey to Florida.

HAIRY PIPEWORT: *Lachnocaulon anceps* (Walter) Morong.

In general aspect resembles the preceding but is somewhat smaller and has a hairy flowering stem.

Eriocaulon decangulare

PICKEREL WEED, WAMPEE: *Pontederia cordata* Linnaeus.

Aquatic plant to 3½ ft. above the water. Rootstock horizontal and well down in the mud. A single large glossy-green heart-shaped leaf and a dense spike of purple flowers make this a very attractive plant. The flowers are rather unpleasantly odorous and each lasts but a day. However, due to lengthening of the spike there is an uninterrupted succession of blossoms for weeks. The perianth is tubular, 2-tipped and divided into 6 unequal lobes. The middle lobe of the upper lip has two yellow spots at base within. Stamens 6, 3 opposite each lip.

Swamps and pond margins, rare in the mountains. Summer. Nova Scotia to Florida.

THALIA: *Thalia dealbata* Roscoe.

A tall somewhat Cannalike perennial from thick roots. Leaves large, to 18 in. long, lanceolate or wider and whitened on both surfaces. Flower has 3 minute sepals, 3 short petals and a purple lip ½ in. long. Fruit 3-celled. Rare.

Wet margins and ditches. Summer. Southeastern South Carolina and Missouri to Texas.

Mayaca aubletii Michaux. An elongate, creeping, mosslike plant with numerous, very small linear leaves. Flowers solitary, 3-parted axillary and pale violet.

Muddy or shallow margins, Coastal Plain. Spring. Virginia to Florida.

YELLOW-EYED GRASS: *Xyris caroliniana* Walter.

Perennial from a bulblike base; leaves linear, less than ¼ in. wide, spirally twisted and to 18 in. long; flower stalk leafless and topped by an ovoid head of tough, brownish scales from which emerge delicate, 3-parted yellow flowers, one or few at a time.

Savannahs and wet open margins, Coastal Plain. Summer. Nova Scotia to Florida. Several other species are in the Carolinas.

9

COLICROOT: *Aletris farinosa* Linnaeus.

From a rosette of short, thick, firm basal leaves a 15–30 in. flowering stem arises bearing numerous small white flowers showing a granulate surface.

Marshes and wet margins. Spring and summer. New England to Florida.

A. aurea Walter is a somewhat smaller, yellow-flowered form limited to the Coastal Plain.

Wet open places. Spring and summer. North Carolina to Florida.

GREENBRIER: *Smilax smallii* Morong.

A high-climbing woody perennial with usually spineless stems and woody, tuberous roots. Leaves lanceolate or wider, glossy or shining green especially above. Flowers small, green and in clusters from the leaf axes. Berry black and 1-seeded.

Woods and margins, mostly Coastal Plain. Summer. Virginia to Florida and west.

INDIAN CUCUMBER ROOT: *Medeola virginiana* Linnaeus.

A perennial from crisp, white rhizomes. Stem to 18 in. high and with usually 2 whorls of leaves, several in the lower, 3 in the upper. Flowers terminal, on slender stalks, yellowish, with purple stamens. Fruit a blue berry.

Rich woodlands and edges of bays, bogs and pocosins. Spring. Nova Scotia to Georgia.

SPECKLED WOOD LILY: *Clintonia umbellata* (Michaux) Morong.

A rhizome bearing perennial with 2–4 rather large oblong, basal leaves to 10 in. long and conspiciously veined. Flower stalk to 1 ft. high terminated by a cluster of whitish flowers speckled with purple or brown. Berries blue.

Rich moist woods, mountains and upper Piedmont. Spring. New Jersey to Georgia.

FLY POISON: *Amianthium muscaetoxicum* (Walter) Gray.

Bulbous perennial to 3 ft. tall. Leaves mostly basal, blades elongate to 1½ ft. long and ½ in. wide. Flowers borne in a terminal raceme which is at first pointed at the summit but becomes cylindric. Sepals and petals white and undifferentiated. Stamens 6; ovary deeply 3-parted.

Open woods and clearings. Summer. New York to Florida.

CROW POISON: *Zigadenus densus* (Desrousseaux) Fernald.

A similar appearing plant with somewhat narrower leaves, an obscure gland at the base of each sepal and petal and a conical ovary which is barely 3-lobed.

Low woods and savannahs, Coastal Plain. Spring. Virginia and south.

TROUT LILY: *Erythronium americanum* Ker.

A small bulb-bearing herb with two dark green fleshy leaves mottled with purple. Flower is solitary, yellow and usually nodding. Flower color sometimes varies. Tends to grow in small colonies.

Low, moist woodlands, mountains and Piedmont. Early spring. Nova Scotia to Georgia.

SPRING STARFLOWER: *Ipheion uniflorum* Rafinesque.

Low perennial plant from deep-seated bulb and characterized by an onionlike odor. Leaves linear, flattened and somewhat whitish. Flowering stem to 8 in. high and with two dry bracts at about midpoint. Flowers about 1½ in. across. Sepals and petals similar, widely spreading and bluish. Introduced from Argentina and established in some localities as a weed. Spring.

PINE LILY, FLAME LILY, SOUTHERN RED LILY:
Lilium catesbaei Walter.

Stem to 3 ft. high, from small bulb composed of several narrow fleshy scales. Leaves alternate, narrow, pointed up the stem and progressively smaller upward. Flower solitary, erect and about 4 in. in diameter. Perianth segments similar, red, recurved and widely spreading, narrowed toward the base into a claw, becoming paler and purple spotted. Stamens 6; capsule 1½ in. long.

This disappearing species is native to low pinelands and blooms in summer. North Carolina to Louisiana.

CAROLINA LILY: *Lilium michauxii* Poiret.

Similar to Catesby's Lily; leaves oblanceolate, 1 in. or more wide and in whorls; flowers nodding, usually several to many on a stalk.

Dry woods of the Coastal Plain. Summer. Virginia to Louisiana.

TURK'S-CAP LILY: *L. superbum* Linnaeus.

Plant to 6 ft. tall from underground scaly bulb. Leaves lanceolate, less than 1 in. wide and in whorls. Flowers one to several, nodding, segments much recurved and orange with purple spots.

Moist to wet clearings and openings, most abundant in the mountains. Summer. New Brunswick to Florida.

FALSE LILY OF THE VALLEY: *Maianthemum canadense* Desfontains.

Low, erect perennial from slender rhizome; stem to 6 in. tall, bearing usually 2 broadly ovate, sessile, entire leaves and about 1 in. long raceme of small white flowers each made up of 2 sepals, 2 petals, 4 stamens and 1 pistil.

Rich, moist woods, mountains and very upper Piedmont. Late spring. Labrador to Georgia.

SOLOMON'S SEAL: *Polygonatum biflorum* (Walter) Elliott.

Stalk usually arching and 2 ft. or more high arising from a horizontal knotty rhizome on which the stalks of previous years have left their fancied Solomon's seal-shaped scars. Leaves narrowly oval and pointed at the tips, alternate, smooth but with prominent veins and 2-ranked. Flowers are bell-shaped, ½–¾ in. long, greenish-cream and hang in pairs from the leaf axils. Perianth of 6 short lobes encircling 6 stamens. Fruit a globular blue-black berry.

Rich moist woods. Spring. New England to Florida.

P. canaliculatum (Muhlenberg) Pursh is a more robust species with veins very prominently exposed to the tip of the leaf.

P. pubescens (Willdenow) Pursh is distinguished by pubescence on the veins beneath. Both occur in the Piedmont and mountains.

13

FALSE SOLOMON'S SEAL: *Smilacina racemosa* (Linnaeus) Desfontaines.

Unbranched perennial herb to 2 ft. high from elongated, knotty rhizome. Leaves broadly lanceolate to 6 in. long, prominently nerved and short petioled. Flowers cream, less than ¼ in. in diameter and borne in a terminal panicle. Stamens longer than the petals. Fruit a red berry speckled with purple. Edible.

Rich woods, inland, rare along coast. Spring. Nova Scotia to Georgia.

BIRTHWORT, WAKE ROBIN: *Trillium catesbaei* Elliott.

Low perennial herb to 1½ ft. high with stout unbranched stem arising from short tuberlike rhizome. Leaves 3, netted-veined, oval, 2–4 in. long and borne in a whorl at the summit of the stem. Flower solitary, borne terminally but reflexed on slender pedicel and suspended below the leaves. Petals 3, separate, usually rose-colored and recurved. Fruit a ½ in. thick berry.

Moist hardwood slopes, Piedmont. Spring. North Carolina to Georgia.

T. grandiflorum (Michaux) Salisbury is similar except that the flower which is first white but fades pink is raised well above the leaves by the full length of the slender pedicel.

Rich woods, upper Piedmont and mountains. Maine to Georgia.

WOOD TRILLIUM: *Trillium discolor* Wray.

In general this species is similar in growth habit to the two preceding species. Leaves broad, oval to ovate in outline and mottled green. Flower sessile and erect. Petals broadest above the middle, rounded at the apex and greenish-yellow in color.

Rich woods and bluffs, infrequent. Spring. North Carolina to Georgia.

SESSILE TRILLIUM: *Trillium viride* Beck.

A rare trillium with very local occurrences recorded in the mountains and Piedmont of the Carolinas, and west.

T. cuneatum Rafinesque is similar in appearance but has maroon or purplish brown flowers and is much more common.

Rich woods, Piedmont and mountains, and local on the southern Coastal Plain of South Carolina. Early spring. New York to Georgia.

In both species the leaves are conspicuously mottled.

NARROW-LEAVED WAKE ROBIN: *Trillium lanceolatum* Bokin.

Similar to preceding in general growth habit. Leaves lanceolate and with an irregular streak of silvery-green through the middle. Flower sessile and erect on the summit of the stem. Sepals green and reflexed; petals about ½ in. longer than the sepals and maroon or greenish.

Wooded bluffs of the upper Coastal Plain. Spring. South Carolina to Florida.

Trilliums are easily propagated from seeds, bulbs or parts of bulbs.

BELLWORT: *Uvularia sessilifolia* Linnaeus.

Forking stem to 1 ft. high from slender rhizome. Leaves 1½–3 in. long, broadly lanceolate, pale beneath and without petiole. Flowers yellowish or straw-colored, ¾ in. long and drooping. Sepals and petals 6, separate and undifferentiated. Fruit a 3-angled capsule.

Rich woods and bluffs, mostly Piedmont and mountains. Spring. New Brunswick to Georgia.

U. perfoliata Linnaeus is a more common species with very short rhizomes and leaves with bases ringing the stem. Rich woods and bluffs, Piedmont and mountains. Spring. Massachusetts to Florida.

SPANISH BAYONET: *Yucca aloifolia* Linnaeus.

An unbranched shrub attaining height to 10 ft. Leaves yellow-green, stiff, dagger-shaped and very sharp pointed with fine-toothed margins.

Coastal dunes and brackish marshes. Summer. North Carolina to Florida.

Y. gloriosa Linnaeus is similar to *aloifolia* but has somewhat longer dark or bluish-green leaves with smooth edges.

Sandy margins, outer Coastal Plain. Summer. North Carolina to Georgia

BEAR GRASS: *Y. filamentosa* Linnaeus.

A woody shrub with leathery, evergreen leaves arising from ground level. Flowers waxy white, 2 in. long and hanging from elevated panicle.

Open or sparsely wooded dry habitats. Late spring. New Jersey to Florida.

REDROOT: *Lachnanthes tinctoria* (Walter) Elliott.

Herbaceous plant to 2½ ft. high from slender underground stems which contain a red juice. Leaves elongate, clustered near base of stem, scattered above. Stem and flower cluster loosely woolly. The name *Lachnanthes* is from the Greek and means wool flower. Flowers about ½ in. long and dingy yellow. Sepals and petals undifferentiated, persistent and tightly enclosing a 3-celled capsule.

Low pinelands and clearings of the Coastal Plain. Summer. Nova Scotia to Florida.

Lophiola americana (Pursh) Wood is similar but has 6 stamens instead of 3 and paler colored roots.

17

STARGRASS: *Hypoxis hirsuta* (Linnaeus) Coville.

Small perennial herb reaching a height of 16 in. Leaves grasslike, hairy and arising from a bulbous base. Flowers one to several on a leafless stalk, usually opening one at a time, 6-parted and with 6 stamens, bright yellow within, paler and hairy without, to 1 in. across. Fruit a capsule which at maturity contains a few rounded black seeds with fine surface markings.

This species occurs in open woods and borders, and two additional species occur in the Coastal Plain. They are easily cultivated in suitable locations.

Late spring and summer. Eastern United States and adjacent Canada.

ATAMASCO LILY, FAIRY LILY, CULLOWHEE: *Zephyranthes atamasco* (Linnaeus) Herbert.

Broad, grasslike, shining leaves and a flowering stalk from 6–10 in. high arise from an underground bulb. A single, 6-parted, lilylike white flower from 2–3 in. in diameter is borne in an upright position on the stem. Flower turns pinkish with age. Stamens 6.

Sizable colonies of these bright flowers may be encountered in moist grassy places or rich open woods. Their abundance in some areas results in their being marketed, sometimes under the name "Wild Easter Lily." These beautiful plants may be easily transplanted to a moist or swampy wild garden. Spring. Piedmont and Coastal Plain. Virginia to Alabama.

DWARF CRESTED IRIS: *Iris cristata* Aiton.

Stem not over 6 in. high from stringy and knotty rhizome. Leaves green, lanceolate and from ½–1 in. across. Sepals somewhat recurved, broadest of the flower parts and with three parallel crested flutes marked with yellow and white. Petals more or less upright. Style branches petaloid and arching over the stamens.

Rich woods, banks and bluffs. Spring. Maryland to Georgia.

DWARF IRIS, *I. verna* Linnaeus.

Similar but has whitish-green leaves less than ½ in. wide and no crested flutes on the sepals.

Gravelly, acid soil in full sun. Spring. Pennsylvania to Georgia.

SOUTHERN BLUE FLAG: *Iris virginica* Linnaeus.

Stems 1½–2 ft. high from stout rhizomes. Leaves green, about 1 in. wide and somewhat shorter than the stems. Flowers 2–3 in. across and pale lilac to violet, or occasionally white. Sepals, largest of the flower parts, petaloid and with yellow blotch at base which is downy. Sepals and petals purple-veined. Fruit a many-seeded capsule.

Swamps, roadside ditches and wet openings, mainly Coastal Plain. Early summer. Virginia to Florida.

BURMANNIA: *Burmannia capitata* (Gmelin) Martius

A 2–6 in. high scale-leaved slender, unbranched annual bearing several very small cream-colored flowers at summit.

Wet weedy margins, Coastal Plain. Summer and fall. North Carolina to Florida.

B. biflora Linnaeus is a slightly larger form bearing two blue or purplish 3-winged flowers.

Wet margins, ditches and savannahs, Coastal Plain. Summer and fall. Virginia to Florida.

BLUE-EYED GRASS: *Sisyrinchium albidum* Rafinesque.

Low, slender, often tufted perennial up to about 1½ ft. high. Leaves linear, grasslike and mostly basal. Flowering stem somewhat flattened and winged on either side with narrow leaflike appendages. Flowers about ¾ in. across, blue with a yellowish eye; sepals and petals nearly alike. Fruit a globular capsule. Several other species occur here.

Grassy or sandy places. Summer. New York to Georgia.

BLACKBERRY LILLY: *Belamcanda chinensis* (Linnaeus) De Candolle.

An Irislike introduction from Asia to 30 in. high from thick rhizome. Flowers showy, 2½ in. wide, orange spotted with red, on leafless stalk. Fruit a capsule with wall that recurves at maturity exposing an arrangement of glossy black, fleshy seeds so that the whole structure resembles a Blackberry.

Old homesites and roadsides, mostly Piedmont. Summer. New England, south and west.

GRASS-PINK: *Calopogon pulchellus* (Salisbury) R. Brown.

A slender orchid bearing one or two grasslike leaves and two to several showy pink or rose-purple flowers that open successively up the stem.
Savannahs and pinelands, Coastal Plain and mountain meadows.
Spring and summer. Virginia to Florida.
Two other species are limited to the Coastal Plain.

ROSE POGONIA: *Pogonia ophioglossoides* (Linnaeus) Ker.

Another orchid similar in size, color and habitat to the preceding. Usually single flowered.

SPREADING POGONIA: *Cleistes divaricata* (Linnaeus) Ames.

Also of similar size, color and habitat. Single flowered; the sepals are long, narrow, brownish purple and widely spread.

PINK LADY'S SLIPPER, MOCCASIN FLOWER: *Cypripedium acaule* Aiton.

Plant consists of coarsely fibrous root system, two basal leaves and, when present, a flowering stem up to 1 ft. high. Leaves narrowly oval, thinly pubescent, pale beneath and very prominently veined. Flower solitary on a pubescent stalk. Sepals and lateral petals yellowish or brownish-green, lowest petal or lip much inflated and moccasin-shaped or saclike, pink in color with conspicuous darker veins.

Woodlands, near pines, where the soil is sandy, well aerated and strongly acid. Spring.
Newfoundland to South Carolina and Alabama.

21

YELLOW LADY'S SLIPPER: *Cypripedium calceolus* Linnaeus, variety *parviflorum* (Salisbury) Fernald.

A leafy stalk to 2 ft. high arises from coarsely fibrous roots. Leaves narrowly ovate and pointed. Flower solitary, or sometimes two. Sepals and lateral petals purple-brown, lowest petal, or lip, inflated, yellow and 1½ in. long.

The species occurs in Europe and Asia and only a varietal difference is recognized in the plants growing in North America.

Rich, wooded, mountain slopes. Late spring. Newfoundland to Georgia.

LARGE WHORLED POGONIA: *Isotria verticillata* (Michaux) Rafinesque.

Perennial to 1 ft. high topped by a whorl of 5–6 entire leaves. Flower mostly solitary, terminal and inconspicuous. Sepals greenish-purple, very slender and twice as long as petals. Petals greenish-yellow, lip streaked with purple. Fruit a capsule.

Rich, acidic woods throughout, but infrequent. Spring. Maine to Florida.

SHOWY ORCHIS: *Orchis spectabilis* Linnaeus.

A tuberous rooted perennial with 2 large basal leaves, each to 8 in. long, prominently veined and rather fleshy. Flowers several on stem to 15 in. high, each flower from axil of small stem leaf. Flowers 1–1½ in. long, showing pink, purple and white, orchid-shaped and with twisted spur. Rich, moist woods, mountains and upper Piedmont. Spring. New Brunswick to Georgia.

RATTLESNAKE PLANTAIN: *Goodyera pubescens* (Willdenow) R. Brown.

A perennial from thick fibrous roots giving rise to 3–7 ovate basal leaves to 3 in. long, veined and cross veined in white. Flower stalk to 15 in. high and in its upper portion rather densely packed with small waxy-white flowers

Moist woodlands, mostly mountains and Piedmont. Summer. Newfoundland to Georgia.

BLAZING STAR, FAIRY WAND:*Chamaelirium luteum* (Linnaeus) Gray.

An evergreen rosette-former with elliptic to oblong leaves to 8 in. long, entire and rather fleshy. A plant produces either staminate or pistilate flowers on a flower stalk to 2 ft. high. Flowers white, many to the stem and progressively smaller upward. Fruit a 3-celled capsule.

Rich woods, infrequent toward the coast. Summer. Massachusetts to Florida and west.

ORANGE FRINGED ORCHID: *Habenaria ciliaris* (Linnaeus) Robert Brown.

Stems 1–3 ft. tall, leafy, upper leaves much reduced. Inflorescence a many-flowered raceme of orange flowers. Sepals 3, broadly oval. Lateral petals narrower than the sepals, lip or lowest petal longest of the perianth parts and deeply fringed. A long spur is also present.
Wet thickets and grassy places. Summer. Massachusetts to Florida.

YELLOW FRINGED ORCHID: *H. cristata* (Michaux) Robert Brown.
Wet to moist open woods and grasslands, Coastal Plain. Summer. New Jersey to Florida.

WHITE FRINGED ORCHID: *H. blephariglottis* (Willdenow) Hooker.
Savannahs and boggy places, mostly Coastal Plain. Summer. Newfoundland to Georgia.

PUTTYROOT, ADAM-AND-EVE: *Aplectrum hyemale* (Muhlenberg) Torrey.
A perennial from globose rhizome produced at rate of 1 leaf and 1 rhizome per year, each rhizome connected to the one of the preceding year. Leaf basal, elliptic, rather folded, conspicuously veined, to 5 in. long and produced in the fall. Flower stalk and purplish-brown flowers produced in spring.
Rich woods, mountains and Piedmont. Vermont to Georgia.

CANE-FLY ORCHID: *Tipularia discolor* (Pursh) Nuttall.
A perennial colony former with leaves to 3 in. long arising singly from small solid bulbs, dull green above, purplish beneath, developing in the fall, absent at flowering time in late summer. Flowers several on slender stalk; petals yellowish and very slender; spur longer than petals and also very slender.
Rich moist woods, throughout. Vermont to Georgia and west.

Spiranthes cernua

floridana

SWAMP LADIES' TRESSES: *Spiranthes cernua* (Linnaeus) Richard.

Plant with mostly basal leaves to 10 in. long with little or no pubescence. Stem from 6–15 in. high. Flowers white, compactly borne and without spurs.
Swamps and other low wet places. Late summer. Nova Scotia to Florida.

S. gracilis (Bigelow) Beck is known as Southern Slender Ladies' Tresses. Leaves usually absent at flowering time. Flowers white and in a single spiral up the stem.
Dry, mostly open situations. Late summer. New England to Florida and west.

Variety *floridana* (Wherry) Correll, shown here, has a long, very slender leaf or two present at flowering time, the tip of one is visible to right of stem. This variety reaches the northern limits of its range in the Coastal Plain of North Carolina.

LIZARD'S-TAIL: *Saururus cernuus* Linnaeus.

Perennial herb extensively spreading from aromatic underground stems. Flowering stems from 1½–3 ft. high, jointed and bearing heart-shaped leaves from 2–5 in. long. Each leaf distinctly petioled and without pubescence. Flowers small, white and in slender curving spikes. Sepals and petals lacking; the 6 stamens much overtopping the immature capsule.
Swamps and shallow ponds, except in the mountains. Summer. Quebec to Florida.

WILD GINGER, HEART LEAF: *Hexastylis arifolia* (Michaux) Small.

A pleasantly aromatic, stemless perennial herb with long petioled triangular-cordate leaves. Leaves are 2–4 in. long, thick in texture and mottled green. Light purplish-colored flowers occur at ground level but are usually hidden by the dry leaves and litter of the forest floor. The three persistent sepals are united to form a pitcher-shaped tube about 1 in. long. Petals absent; stamens 12; fruit containing several seeds.

Common in hardwood forests. Early spring. Virginia to Florida.

A related plant, *Asarum canadense* Linnaeus, has one pair of deciduous, roundly heart-shaped, pubescent leaves from a horizontal, barely underground stem. A single short-stalked maroon flower with long, pointed lobes arises between them.

Infrequent, rich woods, mountains and Piedmont. Spring. Quebec to South Carolina.

WILD BUCKWHEAT: *Eriogonum tomentosum* Michaux.

An erect pubescent perennial arising from a basal rosette of elliptic leaves that may all but disappear by flowering time. The basal leaves and later the stem leaves, which appear in whorls of 3 or 4, are densely white or tan pubescent beneath.

Sandhill region. Late summer and fall. South Carolina to Florida.

BUCKWHEAT: *Fagopyrum esculentum* Moench.

An erect plant with arrow-shaped leaves and clusters of small white flowers; occasionally found as an escape along roads and in waste ground.

Eriogonum tomentosum

SMARTWEED: *Polygonum pensylvanicum* Linnaeus.

Weakly erect, branched annual to 5 ft. high. Leaves lanceolate or wider and to 4 in. long. Stems reddish, with prominent joints and peculiar sheathing structures at the bases of the leaves. Flowers small, usually pink and in dense spikes. Petals lacking; sepals 4 or 5 and petaloid; achenes black, smooth and shining.

Wet margins, clearings and fields. Summer and fall. Nova Scotia to Florida.

P. punctatum Elliott. Annual with narrowly lanceolate leaves to 5 in. long which arise from within peculiar sheathing structures at the joints on the stem. Flowers without petals, calyx greenish, glandular dotted and enclosing the 3-sided achene. Flowers small and thinly scattered on the flowering branches. Wet open grounds and swamps. Common throughout.

KNOTWEED: *P. aviculare* Linnaeus.

Hardy, much branched annual or perennial, branches lying flat on the substrate. Leaves bluish green and mostly less than ½ in. long. Flowers from leaf axils and inconspicuous. Homesites, roadsides and street and sidewalk crevices. Common throughout.

Another hardy dweller of above type habitats is *Euphorbia supina* Rafinesque. It has leaves from ¼–½ in. long. They are usually reddish, unequal sided at base and along with the stem have milky juice. Common throughout.

JOINTWEED, SANDHILL HEATHER: *Polygonella americana* (Fischer and Meyer) Small.

A related plant to 3 ft. high with numerous short, leafy branches. Leaves short and widening upward. Flowers toward branch tips, crowded, white and becoming tinted with age. Perennial.

Sandhills. Summer and fall. South Carolina, Georgia and Alabama.

LADIES'-EARDROPS: *Brunnichia cirrhosa* Banks.

A partly woody tendril-bearing vine with deciduous, alternate, ovate leaves to 4½ long. Flowers small, greenish and in short racemes. With maturity the petaloid calyx becomes about 1 in. long, pink, 5-lobed and flattened toward base. Rare.

Low woods and streambanks, Coastal Plain. Summer. South Carolina south and west.

SORREL, RED SORREL, SHEEP SORREL: *Rumex hastatulus* Baldwin.

An often troublesome weed of waste places and run-down, sour soils. This plant and the closely related species often form the dominant cover over extensive areas in early spring. Leaves 1–2 in. long and usually with two divergent lobes toward the base. They are pleasantly sour and sometimes used in salads. Flowers small, perfect or unisexual; petals lacking; achene 3-winged.

Early spring. Massachusetts to Florida.

R. Acetosella Linnaeus, has slender spreading rootstocks and achenes that are wingless when mature. Naturalized from Europe.

POKEBERRY, POLKWEED, INDIAN POLK: *Phytolacca americana* Linnaeus.

Coarse plant 6 ft. or more tall, arising from a greatly enlarged root. All parts of the plant are poisonous except the very young leafy shoots which are often eaten when properly cooked. Leaves entire, narrowly ovate, 4–12 in. long, glabrous. Stems smooth becoming reddish-purple. Flowers small, in racemes to 6 in. long. Sepals 5, white; petals obscure. Fruit a dark purple berry ripening in fall which, in either the fresh or dry state, is relished by birds.

Clearings and open woods. Summer. Maine to Florida.

SPRING BEAUTY: *Claytonia virginica* Linnaeus.

Low, sprawling plant from small deeply buried tuber. Stem producing one pair of opposite, long, narrow leaves and a loose raceme of ½ in. wide, pink flowers with deeper colored veins. Sepals 2; petals 5. Transplants easily to suitable locations.

Damp rich woods and borders. Early spring until summer. Eastern United States and adjacent Canada.

COTTONWEED: *Froelichia floridana* (Nuttall) Moquin-Tandon.

Tall, grayish, cottony annual with opposite, entire, narrow leaves, and not many of them. Flowers rather hidden in densely cottony heads. Fruit dry and 1 seeded.

Dry, sandy fields and margins, Coastal Plain. Summer. Mid-North Carolina and south.

SANDWORT: *Arenaria caroliniana* Walter.

Densely matted low evergreen arising from a deep taproot, The low, rounded, 2–5 in. wide cushion-shaped mats are often half or more covered by drifting sand. Stems short, branched and bristly with firm, linear to lanceolate leaves. Flowering stems slender and to 8 in. high, branched toward the summit and several flowered. Flowers white, ¾ in. wide, including 5 sepals and 5 separate petals.

Rocky or sandy woods, mostly Coastal Plain. Virginia to Georgia.

A. serpyllifolia L. has paired leaves each less than ¼ in. long, white flowers less than ¼ in. wide and is widely distributed in lawns, margins and pastures from Maine to Florida. Introduced.

28

PINK: *Dianthus armeria* Linnaeus.

Low tufted perennial to 1 ft. high with stems reclining at the base. Leaves opposite, keeled, narrowly lanceolate and to ¾ in. long. Flowers one to few per stem and about ½ in. in width. Petals 5, roseate, with dark line at base and toothed at the tip. Naturalized from Europe.

Occasional in fields and along roadsides in the mountains. Summer. New England to South Carolina.

SWEET WILLIAM: *D. barbatus* Linnaeus.

Glabrous perennial to 15 in. tall. Leaves opposite, lanceolate and to 2 in. long. Flowers pink, or varying from red to whitish. An introduced Old World ornamental, sometimes escaped.

CORN COCKLE: *Agrostemma githago* Linnaeus.

A hairy annual to 30 in. tall. Leaves opposite, narrow and to 5 in. long. Solitary flower arising from each stem joint; calyx cylindric with 5 slender lobes longer than the tube; petals 5, red and ¾ in. long.

An introduction from Europe now widespread to grain fields and waste areas, mountains and Piedmont. Late spring.

MULLEIN PINK: *Lychnis coronaria* (Linnaeus) Desrousseaux.

Similar to Corn Cockle and also an introduction from Europe. It differs mainly in having calyx lobes very much shorter than the calyx tube and shorter and broader leaves.

Escaped to margins and waste places. Late spring. Virginia, North Carolina and Kentucky.

STANDING CYPRESS: *Gilia rubra* (Linnaeus) Heller.

A mostly unbranched biennial to 3 ft. high, introduced from the southwest. Leaves alternate and divided into narrow segments. The 5-lobed red flowers have long corolla tubes that are yellow within.

Dry, sandy soil. Summer. North Carolina to Texas. Often planted. A Phlox relative.

CAROLINA PINK: *Silene caroliniana* Walter.

Perennial herb 2–8 in. high from stout taproot and tending to form small mats. Basal leaves 2–4 in. long, oblanceolate, tapering to the petiole and densely grayish pubescent on both sides. Stem leaves 2–3 pairs and narrower. Flowers about 1 in. across, white or pink. Petals 5, barely notched at apex, each extended into a long claw which continues separately to the bottom of the tubular calyx. Styles 3.

Rocky, open woods. Spring. North Carolina and South Carolina.

FIRE PINK: *S. virginica* Linnaeus.

A very showy crimson flowered perennial with slender oblanceolate leaves and a height to 18 in.

Open woods, banks and rocky slopes, mostly mountains and Piedmont. Spring. New Jersey to Georgia and Alabama.

BOUNCING BET, SOAPWORT: *Saponaria officinalis* Linnaeus.

Resembles Carolina Pink but is an introduction from the Old World, has only 2 styles and occurs along roadsides and on waste ground.

GIANT CHICKWEED: *Stellaria pubera* Michaux.

A low spreading perennial with 5 very deeply cleft, white petals. Leaves are elliptic to obovate and paired.

Rich woods, mostly mountains and Piedmont. Spring. New Jersey to Florida.

S. media (Linnaeus) Cyrillo is the much smaller European introduction which grows as a common weed in lawns, fields and roadsides.

FRAGRANT WATER LILY: *Nymphaea odorata* Aiton.

Aquatic perennial herb from thick, branched rhizomes. Leaves 6–10 in. long, nearly orbicular with a V-shaped sinus at the point of attachment, commonly red or purple beneath and floating. Flower solitary, 2–4 in. wide, white, pink, yellow, or blue, opening for a few hours each morning for several days. Petals numerous. Fruit maturing under water.

Ponds in or near the Coastal Plain. Spring and summer. New Jersey to Florida.

YELLOW POND LILY: *Nuphar luteum* (Linnaeus) Sibthorp and Smith.

Aquatic from large rhizome with submersed, floating, or emersed cordate or longer leaves and yellow flowers borne singly. Spring. Piedmont and Coastal Plain.

WATERSHIELD: *Brasenia schreberi* Gmelin.

An aquatic with floating elliptic leaves to 4 in. long that are gelatinous beneath. Flowers brownish-purple and barely 1 in. broad.

Lakes and ponds. Summer. Nova Scotia and south.

FLOATING HEART: *Nymphoides aquatica* (Walter) Kuntze.

A glabrous perennial aquatic with floating, roundly heart-shaped leaves to 3 in. long. Flowers white, in clusters and appearing to arise from petiole at base of leaf.

In quiet water, Coastal Plain. Summer. New York to Florida.

FANWORT: *Cabomba caroliniana* Gray.

Underwater aquatic with long stems and opposite, fan-shaped leaves finely divided into many segments. White flowers about ½ in. wide and 2–3 abortive leaves are born at tip of stem.

Slow streams and ponds, mostly Coastal Plain. Summer. New Jersey to Florida.

WOOD ANEMONE: *Anemone lancifolia* Pursh.

Perennial herb to 1 ft. high from crisp, white, horizontal rhizome. Leaves compound, each consisting of usually three lanceolate leaflets coarsely toothed along the margin. Basal leaf solitary, long petioled and arising from the rhizome. Basal and whorled stem leaves 3-parted. Flower solitary, white and 1 in. or more in width. Petals none; sepals petaloid; achenes about ⅛ in. long.

Rich woods along streams and bluffs mostly in the Piedmont. Spring. Pennsylvania to Georgia.

A. quinquefolia Linnaeus is similar but usually has 5 leaflets instead of 3. Upper Piedmont and mountains.

THIMBLEWEED: *A. virginiana* L.

Perennial to 30 in. high with several basal leaves and 3 leaves on main stem just below the flowers, all deeply parted and toothed. Flowers about 1 in. wide and greenish yellow. Fruiting head 1 in. long consisting of many densely woolly brownish achenes. Rich woods and margins, mountains and Piedmont. Spring. Canada to Georgia.

COLUMBINE: *Aquilegia canadensis* Linnaeus.

A perennial to 2 ft. tall with leaves divided into many leaflets, each lobed toward tip. Flowers red and yellow, each petal long spurred. Fruit capsular.

Rich open woods and margins, mostly mountains and Piedmont. Spring. Nova Scotia to Florida.

MONKSHOOD: *Aconitum uncinatum* Linnaeus.

An erect perennial to 3 ft. tall from tuberous roots. Leaves alternate, 3–5 deep lobes, toothed and to 4 in. long. Flowers terminal or from upper leaf axils. Sepals 5, blue, very irregular; petals 2; stamens numerous; pods several seeded. Flowers 1 in. wide.

Rich woods, mountains. Summer. Pennsylvania to Georgia.

BANEBERRY, DOLL-EYES: *Actaea pachypoda* Elliott.

A perennial herb to 20 in. tall with much divided leaves and toothed leaflets. Flowers small, white and in dense, terminal, 1 in. long racemes. By maturity these racemes may become 6 in. long and the stalks of the individual flowers elongate, thicken and turn red. Fruit is a white 2- to 3-seeded berry with apical dark scar.

Rich woods, mountains and scattered locations in the Piedmont. Spring. Canada to Georgia.

WIND FLOWER, RUE-ANEMONE: *Anemonella thalictroides* (Linnaeus) Spach.

Smooth, slender plant 3–6 in. high from a cluster of tuberous roots. Leaves ternately compound, basal, or whorled on flowering stems. Leaflets usually 3-lobed at the apex. Flowers one to several, white, ¾ in. wide. Sepals 5–10 petaloid; petals obsolete. Pistils several, ribbed.

Rich woods and bluffs. Early spring. Eastern half of the United States.

Isopyrum biternatum (Rafinesque) Torrey and Gray is a similar plant with basal and alternate compound leaves with 3-lobed leaflets.

Rich woods, infrequent. Early spring. Ontario to Florida and west.

LIVERLEAF: *Hepatica americana* (De Candolle) Ker.

An herbaceous perennial of the same family with mottled, 3-lobed, evergreen leaves about 2 in. wide and purplish beneath. Blue flowers in early spring.

Rich bluffs and hillsides, Piedmont and upper Coastal Plain. Nova Scotia to Georgia and west.

BLACK COHOSH: *Cimicifuga racemosa* Nuttall.

A coarse perennial with large compound leaves made up of several to many toothed leaflets. Flowers white and in long terminal racemes. Fruits small dry and several seeded.

Rich woods, mountains and Piedmont. Late spring and summer. Southern Canada to Georgia.

BLUE COHOSH: *Caulophyllum thalictroides* (Linnaeus) Michaux.

Similar in name and has compound leaves but the leaflets are bluntly 3-lobed and not toothed. The flowers are greenish-brown and borne in a short terminal arrangement.

Rich woods and coves, mountains. Spring. New Brunswick to Georgia.

33

LEATHER-FLOWER: *Clematis viorna* Linnaeus.

A barely vinelike herbaceous perennial with pinnate leaves made up of 3–7 leaflets and leaf stalks that may become clasping or twining. Leaflets ovate. Flowers mostly solitary 1 in. long and purplish; sepals 4 and petaloid, petals lacking; stamens several. Fruit consists of achenes with long plumose tips.

Moist woods and borders, mostly Piedmont and mountains. Late spring and summer. Pennsylvania to Georgia.

C. crispa Linnaeus, very similar but with bractless pedicels and mostly on the Coastal Plain. Late spring and summer. Virginia to Georgia.

VIRGIN'S BOWER, DEVIL'S DARNING NEEDLE: *Clematis virginiana* Linnaeus.

A perennial climbing vine, climbing partly by means of curling petioles. It forms a heavy leafy top or bower. Leaves 3-foliate, leaflets thin, ovate and sparingly toothed. Flowers creamy-white and in clusters. Sepals petaloid. Achenes with long plumose tips.

Moist woods and borders, mostly Piedmont and mountains. Summer. Quebec to Georgia.

BUTTERCUP: *Ranunculus sardous* Crantz.

Annual to 1½ ft. high and freely branched above. Basal leaves several, 3-lobed or 3-parted and each division also additionally lobed. Stem leaves fewer, smaller and more divided. Flowers numerous, long peduncled and about ¾ in. wide. Petals five, glistening yellow; stamens numerous. Fruit numerous small achenes with tiny hook on one side. Introduced from Europe.

Low open ground. Summer. Virginia to Georgia.

Among the several native species are *R. recurvatus* Linnaeus, a leafy perennial with smooth, hooked achenes, and *R. abortivus* Linnaeus, a very small flowered annual with broadly heart-shaped basal leaves and dissected stem leaves. The achenes are smooth and barely beaked. Both are widespread.

UMBRELLA MAGNOLIA: *Magnolia fraseri* Walter.

Twigs glaucous, leaves deciduous and to 15 in. long, auricled at the base and clustered at the ends of the twigs so as to form an umbrellalike appearance. Flowers yellow or white.

Rich woods, mountains. Late spring. Virginia to Georgia.

UMBRELLA MAGNOLIA: *M. tripetala* Linnaeus.

A large tree with glabrous twigs and somewhat smaller leaves which are green and pubescent beneath and clustered at the ends of twigs. Leaves lacking basal lobes. Flowers white, 6 in. in diameter.

Rich moist woods, Piedmont and mountains. Pennsylvania to Georgia.

Magnolia fraseri

35

GREAT LEAF MAGNOLIA: *Magnolia macrophylla* Michaux.

Small to medium-sized tree with large pubescent twigs and broadly oblanceolate deciduous leaves cordately lobed at the base and whitened beneath. Leaves to 40 in. long. Flowers, the largest in North America, are about 16 in. across, white and fragrant. Petals broad. Formerly found in Coastal Plain woodlands but now scarce even in cultivation. Late spring. North Carolina to Louisiana.

CUCUMBER TREE: *M. acuminata* Linnaeus.

Leaves elliptic, 6-10 in. long, green on both sides, deciduous and scattered along the twigs. Flowers greenish-yellow, 4-6 in. wide.

Rich woods, mostly in the uplands. Spring. New York to Georgia.

SCHISANDRA: *Schisandra glabra* (Brickell) Rehder.

A very rare twining, deciduous, woody vine. Leaves alternate, narrowly elliptic, barely toothed, glabrous, to 5 in. long, much pointed at each end, and on well-developed petioles. Flowers axillary, solitary, small, on long slender supports and either male or female on same plant. Both types are greenish with red centers. Fruit a crowded cluster of red berries each ¼ in. long, with 1 or 2 seeds.

Rich woods, mostly lower Coastal Plain. Spring. North Carolina to Florida and west to Mississippi and Tennessee.

Akebia quinata (Houttuyn) Dene is a semievergreen, woody, twining vine with alternate leaves consisting usually of 5 slightly obovate entire, glabrous leaflets. Flowers small, greenish or brownish, 3-parted and on a particular vine all either staminate or all pistillate. Fruit seldom formed, but fleshy and 2–3 in. long. Introduced from the Orient as an ornamental and sometimes escaped.

CAROLINA MOONSEED, CORALBEADS: *Cocculus carolinus* (Linnaeus) De Candolle.

Perennial woody vine with ovate or 3-lobed entire broad-based leaves and small yellow-green inconspicuous flowers that are either staminate or pistillate per vine. Berry coral red and ¼ in. wide.

Woods, margins and waste areas, Piedmont and Coastal Plain. Summer. North Carolina to Florida.

MOONSEED: *Menispermun canadense* Linnaeus.

Differs by having somewhat larger leaves, some with as many as 5 or 7 lobes, and blue berries.

Low woods. Summer. Widely scattered from Canada to Georgia.

MAGNOLIA BAY, SWEET BAY: *Magnolia virginiana* Linnaeus.

Usually a shrub with semievergreen elliptic leaves about 4 in. long, whitened beneath and fragrant.
Low woods, Coastal Plain. Spring. Massachusetts to Florida.

SOUTHERN MAGNOLIA: *M. grandiflora* Linnaeus.

Large evergreen tree with dark green coriaceous leaves glabrous, rusty or covered with a dense purplish pubescence beneath and 6–8 in. long. Flowers white and about 6 in. across. Rich moist woods mostly in the Coastal Plain. Late spring. Virginia and south. Widely grown for ornament. State flower of Louisiana and Mississippi.

RED BAY: *Persea borbonea* (Linnaeus) Spreng.

A medium sized evergreen tree with dark green, entire, elliptic-leaves, pubescent or nearly smooth beneath. Flowers green and inconspicuous. Drupes ⅓ in. long, bluish black and on red peduncles. Low woods, mostly Coastal Plain. Spring. Delaware to Florida and Texas. Leaves and fruits aromatic.

OTHER BAYS:

Southern Magnolia is also known as Bull Bay. *Gordonia lasianthus* (Linnaeus) Ellis of low woods, bays and pocosins of the Coastal Plain is Loblolly Bay and the cultivated *Laurus nobilis* Linnaeus provides the Bay leaves of commerce

Red Bay is related to such other fragrants as *Sassifras albidum* (Nuttall) Nees; Spice Bush *Lindera benzoin* (Linnaeus) Blume (both wide ranging); and Pond Spice *Litsea aestivalis* (Linnaeus) Fernald, the rare shrub of wet woods, bays and pocosins, Coastal Plain. North Carolina to Florida.

PAPAW, PAWPAW: *Asimina triloba* (Linnaeus) Dunal.

Deciduous shrub or occasionally small tree to 4–5 in. in diameter. Leaves 6–10 in. long, short acuminate at apex, widest about the middle, and gradually narrowed toward the base. Flowers 1–1½ in. wide with 6 brownish-purple petals in 2 whorls, appearing before the leaves. Fruit fleshy, edible, and about 1½ in. thick and from 2–6 in. long; ripens in late summer and is yellowish-brown, soft and fragrant. Seed flattened, about 1 in. long.

Rich low woods, especially along streams. New York to Florida.

DWARF PAPAW: *A. parviflora* (Michaux) Dunal.

Shrub seldom over 4 ft. high with ovate leaves and fruit less than half the size of the large pawpaw.

Woodlands, Piedmont and Coastal Plain. Virginia to Florida.

TULIP TREE, YELLOW POPLAR: *Liriodendron tulipifera* Linnaeus.

Large deciduous tree with gray bark and glabrous leaves to 6 in. wide and equally long. Flowers green to yellow with orange; stamens many; pistils many; fruit winged.

Rich or moist woods, throughout. Spring. Vermont to Florida.

DUTCHMAN'S BREECHES: *Dicentra cucullaria* (Linnaeus) Bernhardi.

Low, succulent perennial producing clusters of white bulblets. Leaves glabrous and much divided, the ultimate segments narrow. Flowers few and white with two conspicuous upward pointing spurs. Fruit a capsule. Plants flower in early spring, then disappear.

Rich moist woods, mountains and scattered locations in the Piedmont. Quebec to Georgia.

WILD RADISH: *Raphanus raphanistrum* Linnaeus.

A coarse annual to 18 in. high from stout taproot. Leaves much lobed on sides, lobes smaller toward base, basal ones to 6 in. long. Flowers yellow, fading paler with age. Fruits cylindric, 1 in. long and constricted between the 3–8 seeds. Native of Eurasia.

Fields, roadsides and waste places, throughout. Spring. Quebec to Florida.

Warea cunefolia (Muhlenberg) Nutall is an erect, branched annual to 15 in. high with oblanceolate entire leaves to 1½ in. long. Flowers pale pink and in short terminal clusters. Pod slender, to 2 in. long, curved and on long stalk.

Dry sandhills. Summer. North Carolina to Florida.

MAYAPPLE, MANDRAKE: *Podophyllum peltatum* Linnaeus.

Plant about 1 ft. high from a long running underground rootstock. Large, 5- to 7-lobed, peltate leaves arising singly. On flowering stems usually 2 leaves are borne from the axil of which a solitary, nodding, white flower from 2–2½ in. across is produced. The sepals fall away very soon after the flower opens leaving the perianth composed of 6–9 rather large separate petals. Stamens twice as many as the petals. Fruit about the size of an egg, yellowish and edible. Other parts of the plant are toxic and used only in drug manufacture.

Low, moist woods. Spring. Quebec to Florida.

UMBRELLALEAF: *Diphylleia cymosa* Michaux.

A rhizomatous herb with 1–3 irregularly and deeply lobed and toothed leaves to 18 in. in diameter. Flowers several ½ in. wide and white; berry small and dark blue.

Rich woods and banks, mountains and very upper Piedmont. Spring. Virginia to Georgia.

TWINLEAF: *Jeffersonia diphylla* (Linnaeus) Persoon.

A perennial with leaves and flowers arising directly from underground rhizome. Leaves 2-parted and to 5 in. long, and with the two parts together almost that broad. Flower solitary, white and overtopping leaves; petals 1 in. long; capsule several seeded.

Rich woods, mountains. Spring. Ontario to Georgia.

CORYDALIS: *Corydalis flavula* (Rafinesque) De Candolle.

A weakly ascending, succulent annual to 1 ft. high. Leaves are glaucous or whitened green and much divided. Flowers yellow, irregular and with saccate base. Fruit an elongate, several-seeded pod.

Low, rich woods and floodplains, mostly mountains and Piedmont. Early spring. New York to Georgia.

SWEET-SHRUB, CAROLINA ALLSPICE, STRAWBERRY-BUSH, APPLE-SHRUB: *Calycanthus floridus* Linnaeus.

Deciduous shrub spreading by underground parts and tending to form small colonies. Leaves oval, 2–4 in. long, pubescent beneath, opposite and borne on brownish twigs. Flowers brownish-purple, sepals and petals undifferentiated, numerous and fragrant. Fruit 2–3 in. long containing several peanut-sized brown seeds.
Rich woods and bluffs. Spring. Pennsylvania to Alabama.

Chimonanthus praecox Link is a similar and closely related ornamental from China and Japan that produces very fragrant yellow flowers very early in spring.

BLOODROOT: *Sanguinaria canadensis.* Linnaeus.

Herbaceous plant arising from a thick horizontal underground stem containing a reddish juice which was used as a dye by the Indians. Leaves circular in outline but usually coarsely lobed, waxy-green above and whitened beneath; veins prominent, with the red sap often showing through. Flower solitary 1–2 in. wide, appearing with the leaves. Sepals 2 but very short-lived; petals 8–12, falling easily. Capsule from 1–2 in. long.
Rich woods and thickets. Early spring. Southern Canada to Florida.

PITCHER PLANT, TRUMPETS, HUNTER'S HORN:
Sarracenia flava Linnaeus.

Yellowish-green perennial, conspicuous because of the 1–2½ ft. high hollow, trumpet-shaped leaves which are winged on one side and have a hood over the open end. Leaves and flower stalks arising from an underground horizontal rootstock. Flower solitary, 2–3 in. across and greenish-yellow throughout. Petals 5, drooping and soon lost. Central part of flower covered by a tough, inverted umbrella-shaped structure which persists as an extension of the capsule.

Wet clearings and savannas, Coastal Plain. Summer. Virginia to Florida.

S. rubra Walter is a smaller plant with very slender leaves and dark red or maroon flowers.

Shaded, acidic, wet margins, Coastal Plain. Spring. Virginia to Florida.

HUNTER'S CUP: *S. purpurea* Linnaeus.

Produces horizontal pitcher-shaped leaves in which it is fancied the wing forms the handle. The opening to the leaf cavity is covered by stiff downward pointing hairs which serve to block the escape of insects that have been lured to the cavity by the usually present water supply. The leaves are reddish-green with prominent redder veins. The petals are purple.

Wet woods and clearings. Summer. Labrador to Florida.

41

HOODED PITCHER-PLANT: *Sarracenia minor* Walter.

Perennial plant seldom over 1 ft. high from a coarsely fibrous horizontal rootstock. Leaves leathery, hollow and with a terminal hood, variegated above with red or purple veins and white or yellowish spots. Flower stalk slightly longer than the leaves. Flower solitary and about 2 in. across. Petals 5, yellow and drooping. Style umbrella-shaped at summit and persistent. Fruit a capsule.

Low open woods, clearings, and roadsides, lower Coastal Plain. Spring. North Carolina to Florida.

SUNDEW: *Drosera capillaris* Poiret.

Very small rosette former catches tiny insects with tentaclelike glandular hairs that produce a sticky secretion. During the summer pinkish flowers are borne on a raised stem.

Wet margins and savannahs, mostly Coastal Plain. Virginia to Florida.

D. intermedia Hayne has a somewhat leafy stem and narrower leaves with much longer petioles and ranges from Newfoundland to Florida.

FALSE GOATSBEARD: *Astilbe biternata* Ventenat.

A coarse perennial with compound leaves; leaflets toothed and the terminal one is 3-lobed. Inflorescence heavy with numerous white flowers and usually drooping; fruits dry and 2-valved; seeds numerous.

Rich wooded slopes, mountains. Early summer. West Virginia to Georgia.

GOATSBEARD *Aruncus dioicus* (Walter) Fernald.

Similar but terminal leaflets are not 3-lobed. Plants bear either staminate flowers only or pistillate flowers only. Flowers are white, the staminate more showy.

Rich woods and bluffs, mountains and upper Piedmont. Summer. New York to Georgia.

CLIMBING HYDRANGEA: *Decumaria barbara* Linnaeus.

A semievergreen, slender, woody vine climbing by aerial roots. Leaves opposite, ovate, thick shining green above and dull beneath, margin entire or barely toothed. Flowers small, dingy white, fragrant and in dense terminal clusters. Petals 7–10; stamens 20 or more. Fruit a small capsule.

Swamps, stream banks and moist woods. Summer. Virginia to Florida.

WILD HYDRANGEA: *Hydrangea arborescens* Linnaeus.

Deciduous shrub seldom over 4 ft. high. Stems weak because of large central pith column. Leaves opposite, ovate, petioled and distinctly toothed and whitish beneath. Flowers in a flat-topped terminal cluster, central ones fertile, marginal ones sterile but showy because of enlarged and petaloid calyx lobes. Petals white and small; stamens several. Fruit a small capsule.

Rich woods and moist bluffs. Summer. New York to Georgia.

OAK-LEAVED HYDRANGEA: *H. quercifolia* Bartram.

A more southern form with larger and lobed leaves and flowers in a panicle to 1 ft. long. A frequently used ornamental.

VIRGINIA WILLOW: *Itea virginica* Linnaeus.

Deciduous shrub 5–10 ft. tall. Leaves alternate, oblong, finely toothed and from 1–3 in. long. Inflorescence of several-to-many terminal racemes. Flowers small, white or occasionally pink. Petals and stamens 5. Fruit a 2-parted, many seeded capsule.

Swamps and wet woods, mostly in the Coastal Plain. Early summer. New Jersey to Florida.

44

MOCK ORANGE, SYRINGA:
Philadelphus inodorus Linnaeus.

Deciduous shrub from 4–8 ft. tall. Leaves opposite, elliptical to ovate, green on both sides, remotely toothed, and from 1½–3 in. long including short petiole. Flowers showy, 1½–2 in. across, borne solitary or not more than three together. Petals 4, white; stamens clustered in the center making the flower appear to be yellow-throated. Fruit a many-seeded capsule.

Rocky bluffs and stream banks. Late spring. Virginia to Florida.

P. coronarius Linnaeus, is the cultivated variety introduced from Europe. These 2 species resemble each other very closely but the latter is more floriferous, bearing from 5–7 flowers together, and is very fragrant.

WITCH HAZEL: *Hamamelis virginiana* Linnaeus.

Deciduous shrub; rarely small tree. Leaves mostly obovate, somewhat pubescent, with a few shallow, rounded teeth and to 3 in. long. Flowers sulphur yellow or darker with 4 long, slender petals. Fruit a capsule about ½ in. long.

Woods and margins, throughout. Late fall. Nova Scotia to Florida.

WITCH ALDER: *Fothergilla gardenii* Murray.

A colony-forming deciduous shrub to 4 ft. high with alternate, elliptic toothed leaves. The showy white flowers appear in advance of the leaves.

Bays, pocosins and savannahs, Coastal Plain. Early spring. North Carolina to Florida.

F. major (Sims) Loddiges is a rare and larger form of the upper Piedmont and mountains.

SHADBLOW, JUNEBERRY: *Amelanchier arborea* (Francois Michaux) Fernald.

Large shrub or tree seldom over 30 ft. high. Leaves alternate, oval, cordate at base and sharply toothed around the margin. Flowers white, 1–1½ in. across and in drooping racemes. Petals 5, long and narrow. Fruit a red berry, edible.

Flowers appear before leaves. Indians associated the blooming of this plant with the movement of shad up streams to spawn.

Rich woodlands and borders. Newfoundland to Florida and westward. Two or three additional species are also native.

CHOKEBERRY: *Aronia arbutifolia* (Linnaeus) Elliott.

Upright shrub from 3–5 ft. tall with pubescent twigs. Leaves deciduous, elliptic or broadest toward the apex, 1–2 in. long, finely toothed, tomentos beneath, and borne in an alternate arrangement. Flower clusters near and at the tips of stems, appearing with the leaves. Petals 5, white and about ¼ in. long. Fruit ¼ in. in diameter, applelike and bright red.

Swamps and wet woods, Coastal Plain. Spring. Nova Scotia to Florida.

A. melanocarpa (Michaux) Elliott is a generally similar shrub but with little or no pubescence on twigs or under side of leaves and with black fruits.

Moist woods, clearings and wet banks, mountains. Spring. Newfoundland to Georgia.

STRAWBERRY: *Fragaria virginica* Duchesne.

Perennial from short rootstock and with long runners. Leaves from base, long petioled and with 3 toothed leaflets. Flowers white and to 1 in. wide. Fruit fleshy, red, sweet and covered with many small seeds.

Woods and borders, mostly mountains and Piedmont. Spring. Newfoundland to Georgia.

46

INDIAN STRAWBERRY: *Duchesnea indica* (Andrews) Focke.

Perennial tufted herb with trailing branches often rooting at the nodes. Leaves 3-foliate and long petioled. Leaflets silky-pubescent, obovate, at the apex and toothed along the margin. Peduncles axillary and slightly longer than the leaves. Flowers ½ in. or more broad with 5 yellow petals. Calyx subtended by toothed bractlets. Stamens and pistils numerous. Fruit red and strawberrylike but insipid.

A widely spread introduction from India. Waste places. Spring. New York to Florida.

BOWMAN'S ROOT, INDIAN PHYSIC: *Gillenia trifoliata* (Linnaeus) Moench.

Herbaceous from a perennial root, branching, 1½–3 ft. high. Leaves trifoliate with subulate stipules. Leaflets lanceolate, short stalked and irregularly serrate. Upper leaves often simple, lanceolate or 3-lobed. Flowers white or pinkish. Petals ½ in. in length, and narrow. Calyx reddish.

Woodlands of Piedmont and mountains. Early summer. Ontario to Georgia.

G. stipulata (Muhlenberg) Baillon is generally similar except for broad, foliacious stipules which makes the leaves appear 5-foliate. New York to Georgia.

FIVE-FINGER: *Potentilla canadensis* Linnaeus.

Perennial from very short rhizome. Stems horizontal or ascending and to a foot or more in length. Leaves of 5 palmately arranged leaflets. Leaflets oblanceolate, toothed and soft-silky. Flowers about ½ in. broad, the first one appearing at the joint above the first well-developed internode. Petals 5, yellow. Stem leaves expanding at flowering time.

Dry woods, thickets and borders. Spring. Nova Scotia to Georgia.

P. simplex Michaux is similar but flowers after the stem leaves are grown. Oldest flowers borne one joint farther away from the base than in above species.

P. recta Linnaeus is an erect perennial to 18 in. high with 5–7 leaflets and flowers borne terminally. Spring and early summer.

AVENS: *Geum canadense* Jacquin.

A perennial with variable, lobed and toothed leaves, the lower pinnate, those in the middle trifoliate, the upper often simple. Flowers white and ½ in. wide; achenes very long beaked with hook or kink at tip.

Moist or alluvial woods, throughout. Summer. New England to Georgia and west.

AGRIMONY, HARVEST-LICE: *Agrimonia parviflora* Aiton.

An erect perennial with black roots. Leaves pinnate with 11–19 principal leaflets. Between the principal leaflets there is one (sometimes two) very tiny leaflet. Flowers less than ½ in. wide and yellow. At maturity flower base is rimmed by stiff, hooked bristles.

Moist or alluvial woods throughout. Summer. New England to Georgia and west.

CUT-LEAVED HAWTHORN: *Crataegus marshallii* Linnaeus.

A somewhat spiny, deciduous shrub to 8 ft. high. Leaves pinnately dissected and to 2 in. long. Flowers white and ½ in. wide. Fruit red and ¼ in. long. Valued as an ornamental.

Woodlands, usually along streams, Coastal Plain and low Piedmont. Spring. Virginia to Florida.

48

WILD PLUM: *Prunus americana* Marshall.

Shrub or small tree to 15 ft. high with reddish-brown bark. Leaves elliptic, 1½–3 in. long, smooth above, pubescent on the veins beneath and toothed. Flowers white, ¾ in. wide; fruit 1 in. long, red, and usually covered with a whitish bloom.

Thickets, margins and stream banks. Early spring. New York to Florida.

CHICKASAW PLUM: *P. angustifolia* Marshall.

A smaller and definitely shrubby plant with a strong tendency to form colonies from underground stems. Leaves lanceolate and from 1–2 in. long. Flowers white and about ½ in. in diameter. Fruit 1 in. long and either red or yellow at maturity.

Margins, roadsides and thickets. Early spring. New Jersey to Florida.

HOG PLUM: *P. umbellata* Elliott.

Plant produces an insipid fruit that is dark purple beneath the whitish bloom and only about ½ in. long. This plant is similar to preceding in most other respects.

Dry woods and borders of the Coastal Plain. Early spring. South Carolina to Florida.

NINEBARK: *Physocarpus opulifolius* (Linnaeus) Maximowicz.

A large deciduous shrub with peeling bark. Leaves ovate and 3-lobed and toothed; flowers white, in broad clusters at twig tips with leaves; capsule 5-celled, many seeded.

Stream banks, cliffs and margins, mountains and Piedmont. Spring. Quebec to Georgia and west.

CHERRY LAUREL: *Prunus caroliniana* Aiton.

Small densely foliated evergreen tree, often used as an ornamental and kept as a shrub by pruning. Leaves rather thick, dark shining green above, elliptical and usually serrated. Flowers small, white and in dense axillary racemes shorter than the leaves. Fruit black, about ⅓ in. in diameter and with thin leathery pulp.

Woods and thickets, lower Piedmont and Coastal Plain. Spring. North Carolina to Florida.

BLACK OR WILD CHERRY: *P. serotina* Ehrhart.

Deciduous tree with elliptic, barely toothed leaves and elongate clusters of white flowers that appear with the leaves. The cherries are black, juicy and on occasional trees tasty. Common now as a weed tree throughout the eastern United States.

WILD CRAB APPLE: *Pyrus angustifolia* Aiton.

Deciduous shrub or small tree, sometimes 15 ft. tall, with thorny branches. Frequently spreads by underground stems to form small colonies. Leaves 1–3 in. long, narrow, rounded at the tips and variously toothed or shallow lobed. Flowers showy and very fragrant, appearing before the leaves. Petals 5, pink or rose. Fruit about 1 in. in diameter and excellent for jelly.

Woods and thicket, Coastal Plain. Spring. New Jersey to Florida.

P. coronaria Linnaeus is the common crab apple in the mountains and Piedmont and has broader leaves with sharp-pointed tips. Spring. New York to Georgia.

WILD ROSE: *Rosa carolina* Linnaeus.

Deciduous, perennial shrub seldom over 2 ft. high. Stems usually armed with slender straight prickles; young shoots with bristles. Leaflets usually 5, narrowly oval, about 1 in. long and toothed. Flower usually solitary, pink, 2 in. across. Petals 5; stamens many. Fruit about ⅓ in. in diameter. It is sometimes transplanted to rock gardens and other suitable places where it seems to thrive and hybridize with cultivated roses.

Upland woods. Late spring. Maine to Florida.

SWAMP ROSE: *R. palustris* Marshall.

Leaves made up of usually 7 leaflets not glandular dotted beneath on canes to 6 ft. high. The stipules are entire or very finely toothed. Sepals are mostly less than 1 in. long and the 5 pink petals are each about 1 in. long. The spines are broad-based, flattened and curved. Stream and pond margins and swamp forests. Late spring. Eastern United States and into Canada.

CHEROKEE ROSE: *Rosa laevigata* Michaux.

Evergreen, rampant climber armed with very stout hooked prickles. Leaves 3-foliate, leaflets about 2 in. long, elliptic and finely toothed. Flowers white, or occasionally rose, 2–3 in. across, fragrant. Petals 5; stamens many. This plant is now said to be a native of China but has long been planted in the South. It has escaped from cultivation in many areas and persists as if native. State flower of Georgia. Spring.

SAND BLACKBERRY: *Rubus cuneifolius* Pursh.

Deciduous perennial shrub producing one or more erect canes heavily armed with sharp spines. Although the plant is a perennial the individual canes are biennial and bear only foliage the first year and both foliage and fruit the last. Leaves usually 3-foliate on spiny petioles, leaflets serrate, widest above the middle, more-or-less rounded at the base. Flowers white, 1 in. in diameter. Petals 5; stamens several. Fruit about ½ in. long.

Sandy clearings and borders, mostly in the Coastal Plain. Spring. Connecticut to Florida.

HARDHACK: *Spiraea tomentosa* Linnaeus.

A deciduous shrub to 4 ft. high with lanceolate or wider leaves that are toothed, hairy beneath and to 2 in. long. Flowers small, many, pink; at stem and branch tips. Fruit a capsule.

Bogs, bays and low margins. Summer. Nova Scotia to the northern borders of South Carolina.

MEADOWSWEET: *S. alba* Du Roi.

Similar to preceding but white flowered, glabrous and from Quebec to the mountains of North Carolina.

MOUNTAIN ASH: *Sorbus americana* Marshall.

A deciduous shrub or small tree with compound leaves consisting of 11–17 leaflets; flowers white and in clusters; fruits orange to red.

Spruce-fir forests, high elevations. Summer. Newfoundland to North Carolina.

A similar European species is used as an ornamental in the Piedmont.

LEAD PLANT, FALSE INDIGO: *Amorpha fruticosa* Linnaeus.

Branching deciduous shrub to 8 ft. tall. Leaves odd-pinnate with from 13–25 leaflets, each from ½–1½ in. long. Flowers small, dull-violet or purple, crowded in 4 in. long terminal racemes. Corolla of one petal wrapped around the stamens and style. Fruit a small, short, 1- or 2-seeded pod.

Rich thickets and stream banks. Early summer. New York to Florida.

Four additional species are listed, among them *A. herbacea* Walter is most widespread and common. It is mostly less than 3 ft. high and has densely pubescent stems, leaves and pods.

Dry fields and woodlands, mostly Coastal Plain.

WILD OR FALSE INDIGO: *Baptisia alba* (Linnaeus) Robert Brown.

Erect perennial herb to 4 ft. high and usually with bluish-green foliage and stems. Leaves 3-foliate. Leaflets ¾–1½ in. long and rounded at the apex. Flowers ¾ in. long, white and raised in conspicuous terminal racemes. Pod cylindric. Dry open woods, mostly on the Coastal Plain. Spring. Virginia to Florida.

INDIGO: *Indigofera caroliniana* Miller.

Similar to the more commonly used introduced species of Colonial Period commerce. A rather slender perennial to 4 ft. high with alternate leaves consisting of 9–15 leaflets. Flowers pinkish and ½ in. long; pods small, 1–3 seeded. The root was the source of dye.

Open, sandy woods, Coastal Plain. Summer. Virginia to Florida.

Baptisia alba   **53**

FALSE INDIGO: *Baptisia bracteata* Muhlenberg.

Low perennial herb usually about 1½ ft. in height and producing a rounded crown. Leaves 3-foliate, 2–3 in. long; leaflets oblanceolate. Flowers cream-colored with darker spots on the large petal, about 1 in. long and borne on recurved racemes that droop below the level of the lowest leaves. Pod about 2 in. long.

Dry, open hardwood forests and adjacent roadsides, Piedmont and upper Coastal Plain. Early summer. Mainly South Carolina and south.

Thermopsis mollis (Michaux) M. A. Curtis is a similar plant but with leaves that are densely pubescent beneath and flattened instead of inflated pods.

Open woods, Piedmont and mountains. Virginia to Georgia.

HORSEFLY WEED: *Baptisia tinctoria* (Linnaeus) R. Brown.

Glabrous bushy herb blackening on drying. Leaves 3-foliate; leaflets obovate. Flowers yellow and in racemes terminating the branches.

Dry woods and clearings. Summer. New York to Florida.

B. perfoliata (Linnaeus) R. Brown has orbicular leaves joined together so that the stem appears to pass through their middle. Solitary yellow flowers are borne in spring followed by inch long inflated pods.

Sandhills, mid-South Carolina to Florida.

PARTRIDGE PEA: *Cassia fasciculata* Michaux.

A branching annual to 2 ft. high, erect or nearly so. Leaves pinnate; leaflets small, oblong and arranged in 8–15 pairs with a cup-shaped gland on the rachis below the lowest pair. Flowers showy, yellow and axillary. Petals ¾ in. long and often with a purple spot toward base. Stamens 10, unequal in length, 4 yellow, 6 purple. Fruit a 1–2 in. long, several-seeded, flattened pod.

Old fields, roadsides and waste ground. Summer. Massachusetts to Florida.

WILD SENSITIVE PLANT: *C. nictitans* Linnaeus.

Generally similar but smaller plant. Flowers less than ½ in. in length. Stamens 5. Pod ½–1 in. long.

Habitat and distribution similar to preceding.

BUTTERFLY PEA: *Centrosema virginianum* (Linnaeus) Bentham.

Twining perennial with 3-foliate leaves and slender pods with long toothpicklike points. Calyx lobes long and slender. A likely ornamental.

Open woods and margins. Summer. Virginia to Kentucky and south.

BUTTERFLY PEA: *Clitoria mariana* Linnaeus.

Less vinelike to erect, having shorter, plump pods containing only 4–5 seeds and calyx lobes that are very, very short.

Open woods and margins. Summer. New York to Illinois and south.

Centrosema virginianum

REDBUD, JUDAS TREE: *Cercis canadensis* Linnaeus.

Deciduous tree to 40 ft. in height. Leaves 2–4 in. long, broadly cordate and entire, usually somewhat broader than long. Flowers appearing before the leaves, rosy-pink, ½ in. long, in small clusters along the twigs or sometimes on older branches and trunks appearing to arise directly from the bark. Fruit of tardily deciduous dark brown pods, 2–4 in. long and ½ in. broad. Seed very hard and small. A much used ornamental. Flowers edible.

Connecticut to Florida.

RATTLEBOX: *Crotalaria spectabilis* Roth.

Erect annual usually less than 3 ft. high. Leaves 1-foliate and broadest near rounded tip, tapered at the base and to 4 in. long. Flowers showy, yellow and about ¾ in. long. Pod much inflated and with 2–5 small seeds. This species has been introduced into this country from the Old World tropics and is widespread. The seeds are poisonous to wildlife.

Fall. Fields and roadsides.

C. retusa Linnaeus is similar except that small green bract at the base of each flower is several times longer than wide.

C. sagittalis Linnaeus. Small pubescent native ascending to 1 ft. tall. Leaves elliptic, to 1 in. long, upper with conspicuous inversely arrow-shaped stipules. Flowers few and yellow. Pod inflated and to 1 in. long. Old fields and margins, mainly Piedmont. Summer.

CORAL BEAN, CHEROKEE BEAN: *Erythrina herbacea* Linnaeus.

Stout erect herb attaining 3 ft. in height with underground perennial rootstock. Leaves 3-foliate, leaflets 2–3 in. long and broadest toward the base. Flowers 1½–2 in. long, bright scarlet, in terminal many-flowered racemes. Fruit a short bean-like pod, tough-shelled and constricted between the 3 or 4 seeds. Seeds bright red with black eye; poisonous.

Thickets and dense margins, mostly near the coast. Late spring. North Carolina to Florida.

LUPINE: *Lupinus diffusus* Nuttall.

Prostrate and diffusely spreading perennial arising from deep taproot. A single plant may form a sort of mat covering an area as much as 3 ft. in diameter. Leaves 1-foliate, oblanceolate, evergreen and conspicuously pubescent. Flowers in erect terminal racemes, blue except for white spots in center. In rare individuals the corollas are magenta and white. Fruits are silky beanlike pods about 1½ in. long.

Dry, sandy woods. Spring. North Carolina to Florida.

L. villosus Willdenow is similar but much more hairy and has pink flowers with reddish purple centers.

L. perennis Linnaeus is erect with 7–11 foliate leaves and blue flowers.

DOLLAR WEED: *Rhynchosia simplicifolia* (Walter) Wood.

Simple-leaved erect herb from ½–1½ ft. tall from perennial root. Leaves about the size and shape of silver dollar and very prominently netted veined. Flowers yellow, less than ½ in. long and borne in terminal headlike racemes. Pods about as long as flowers.

Dry sandy woods and borders, Coastal Plain. Summer. Virginia to Florida.

R. tomentosa (Linnaeus) Hooker and Arnott is erect and 3-foliate with pubescent obovate leaflets from 1–2 in. long and dense racemes of small yellow flowers.

R. difformis (Elliott) De Candolle has trailing stems and rounded leaflets.

BLACK LOCUST: *Robinia pseudoacacia* Linnaeus.

Forest tree becoming 50 ft. or more in height and much sought after because of its strength and great resistance to decay. It is one of the most sought after woods for posts. Leaves deciduous and odd-pinnate. Leaflets 7–15 and oval. Flowers fragrant, white, 3–4 in. long and produced abundantly in many-flowered drooping racemes. Pods flat and 2–3 in. long. Forest tree and ornamental varieties exist.

Late spring. Pennsylvania to Florida.

ROSE ACACIA: *Robinia hispida* Linnaeus.

Stoloniferous, deciduous shrub to 6 ft. tall. Branches strongly beset with dark stiff bristles. Leaves odd-pinnate. Leaflets 7–13, ovate and 1–2 in. long. Flowers showy, about 1 in. long, rose-colored and in short axillary racemes. Fruits bristly but seldom developed. Dry woods, banks and borders. Late spring. Virginia to Georgia.

R. nana Elliott is seldom over 1 ft. high, deciduous, spreads by rhizomes and develops drooping racemes of rose colored flowers.

Sandy or open woods of lower Piedmont and Coastal Plain. Spring. Virginia and south.

SENSITIVE BRIER: *Schrankia microphylla* (Dryander) Macbride.

Curious perennial herb closely related to the true sensitive plants of the genus *Mimosa*. Stems up to 3 ft. long, branched, prostrate or reclining, strongly angled, and beset with sharp, hooked prickles. Leaves bipinnate and composed of 4–8 paired primary divisions each of which has 15–25 pairs of very small leaflets. The leaves are very sensitive and fold-up immediately in response to even slight vibrations and to darkness. Many very small rose-colored flowers are borne in long-peduncled spherical heads. Pods 2–4 in. long, prickly and pubescent.

Dry sandy margins and banks. Summer. Virginia to Florida.

GOAT'S RUE, DEVIL'S SHOE STRING: *Tephrosia virginiana*
(Linnaeus) Persoon.

Perennial herb 1–1½ ft. high from deep roots. Leaves odd-pinnate and made up of from 9–21 leaflets, each narrowly oblong and about 1 in. long. Stem and leaves pubescent. Flowers in short terminal racemes. Corolla about ¾ in. long, standard creamy-yellow, wings and keel pink or rose. Pods 1–2 in. long and soft hairy.

Dry open woods, borders and old fields. Early summer. Massachusetts to Florida.

T. spicata (Walter) Torrey and Gray is a closely related and less conspicuous plant, having a prostrate habit, branching stem, fewer and larger leaves and ascending spikelike inflorescence showing usually one deep purple flower at a time.

Habitat and flowering time as preceding. Piedmont and Coastal Plain.

GROUNDNUT: *Apios americana* Medicus.

An herbaceous twining vine bearing small fleshy tubers (edible). Leaves with 5–7 lanceolate leaflets. Flowers are brownish purple and are crowded on short axillary racemes. Pods 2–4 in. long and several seeded.

Moist margins, throughout. Summer. Canada to Florida.

BEACH PEA: *Strophostylis helvola* (Linnaeus) Elliott.

Weakly climbing herbaceous vine; leaflets 3, ovate and glabrous. Purplish flowers, 2–4, are borne on long stalk from leaf axil. Pods to 4 in. long and several seeded. Seeds woolly.

Beaches and dry or sandy upland soil, Coastal Plain and Piedmont. Summer. Quebec to Florida.

MILK VETCH: *Galactia volubilis* (Linnaeus) Britton.

A prostrate or weakly twining vine with 3-foliate leaves and oblong leaflets to 1½ long. Flowers pinkish-purple and ½ in. long; pods flat and to 1½ in. long.

Dry open woods and margins. Summer. Long Island to Florida.

VETCH: *Vicia caroliniana* Walter.

Trailing or climbing perennial herb to 2 ft. in length. Leaves of 5–9 pairs of ½ in. long elliptic leaflets and with a tendril at the tip of rachis. Flowers white with one blue-tipped petal, ½ in. long and in 1-sided racemes. Pods short.

Woods and thickets. Spring. New York to Georgia.

Among the several other vetches occurring here, two introductions are most familiar.

V. villosa Roth is a larger plant than the above and produces crowded, 1-sided racemes of purplish flowers. Cultivated as a forage crop and spread to roadsides and waste places. Introduced from Europe. Spring.

V. angustifolia Nees produces 1–2 blue or violet flowers in the axils of the upper leaves. This is known as common vetch and is often established on roadsides and waste ground. Introduced from Europe. Spring.

CROWN VETCH: *Coronilla varia* Linnaeus.

European introduction similar to the true vetches but without tendrils, with headlike clusters of pinkish flowers and slender pods constricted between the seeds.

Roadsides and waste areas, throughout. Summer.

SAMSON SNAKEROOT: *Psoralea psoralioides* (Walter) Cory.

A perennial herb to 2 ft. tall from large taproot. Leaves with 3 slender, entire leaflets, each to 1½ in long. Flowers purplish, crowded in well-raised short terminal spikes. Pod short, wrinkled and 1-seeded.

Margins and open woods, lower Piedmont and Coastal Plain. Late spring. Virginia to Florida and west.

WISTERIA: *Wisteria frutescens* (Linnaeus) Poiret.

Twining or straggling deciduous shrub. Leaves odd-pinnate. Leaflets 9–15, 1–2 in. long, ovate to oblong. Flowers ¾ in. long, lilac and in short racemes. Pod about 2 in. long and glabrous. This is a rather inconspicuous plant and not to be confused with the high climbing Asiatic introduction.

Along swamps and streams. Spring. Virginia to Florida.

The common ornamental species, *W. floribunda* (Willdenow) DeCandolle, has about 9 leaflets while *W. sinensis* (Sims) Sweet, usually has 15 or more.

WILD GERANIUM, CRANESBILL: *Geranium maculatum* Linnaeus.

Erect perennial to 2 ft. high from thick rootstock. Leaves 2–3 in. across, mottled and deeply palmately lobed. Flowers about 1 in. across, rose-purple or occasionally white. Fruit about 1 in. long with valves opening from the bottom.

Moist woods, bluffs and stream banks. Spring. Maine to South Carolina.

G. carolinianum Linnaeus is a common weedy annual with smaller and more deeply parted leaves and small pale pink flowers less than ½ in. across.

Widely distributed in dry open spaces. Summer.

TALL YELLOW MILKWORT: *Polygala cymosa* Walter.

Herbaceous biennial reaching a height of 2–3 ft. Leaves 2–5 in. long, linear, pointed, mostly basal and greatly reduced upward. Inflorescence terminal and much branched. Individual racemes erect, numerous and many flowered. Flowers small and bright yellow.

Wet open pinelands and margins, lower Coastal Plain. Summer. Delaware to Florida.

P. ramosa Elliott is a similar appearing but much shorter plant with somewhat broader leaves.

ORANGE MILKWORT: *Polygala lutea* Linnaeus.

A biennial herb usually about 6–8 in. high. Leaves 1–2 in. long, obovate to oblong, rounded at tip, mostly arranged in a basal rosette with those on the stem progressively narrowed and smaller. Flowers bright orange-yellow in a dense headlike raceme. Individual flowers perfect but of very irregular shape. Fruit a small capsule.

Open, wet sandy woods, Coastal Plain. Summer. Long Island to Florida.

DWARF POLYGALA: *Polygala nana* (Michaux) De Candolle.

Plant from 1–6 in. high has a rosette of oblanceolate leaves overtopped by a dense arrangement of greenish-yellow flowers that appear in response to favorable conditions any time during summer or fall.

Open, wet sand, mid-South Carolina to Florida. Rare.

(Sundews in foreground)

FRINGED POLYGALA: *P. paucifolia* Linnaeus.

A low perennial with 2–4 well-developed elliptic leaves to 1½ in. long. Above ground or open flowers purplish, few and about 1 in. long. Fruit a capsule.

Rich mountain woods. Spring. Quebec to Georgia.

MILKWORT: *Polygala polygama* Walter.

A biennial herb to 16 in. tall, usually branching from the base. Leaves alternate and narrow. Flowers pink and in terminal racemes. Nonopening flowers may also be produced underground.

Dry, sandy woods. Summer. New Jersey to Florida.

SPURGE NETTLE: *Cnidoscolus stimulosus* (Michaux) Engelmann and Gray.

An herbaceous perennial with alternate irregularly shaped leaves. Stem and leaves beset with stinging prickles. The flowers are a showy white-white; fruit a 3-celled, 3-seeded capsule.

Sandy woods and abandoned fields, mostly Coastal Plain. Spring and summer. Virginia to Florida.

QUEEN'S DELIGHT, QUEEN'S ROOT: *Stillingia sylvatica* Linnaeus.

Deep-rooted perennial herb from 1–2 ft. tall. Leaves glabrous, broadly lanceolate and serrate with incurved glandular teeth. Flowers green, in spikes, some spikes staminate, others with a few pistillate flowers at the base. Petals lacking. Fruit a 3-celled, 3-seeded capsule.

Dry sandy woods, Coastal Plain. Summer. Virginia to Florida.

Sebastiana ligustrina (Michaux) Mueller is an uncommon deciduous shrub to 7 ft. high with alternate, entire, lanceolate leaves to 1½ in. long and short petioles with 2 glandular stipules at base. Flowers small, greenish, in short racemes with only the lower few pistillate. Petals absent. Fruit a 3-seeded capsule.

Low woods, swamps and stream banks, Coastal Plain. Late spring. Southern North Carolina to Florida.

ROSEMARY: *Ceratiola ericoides* Michaux.

Fragrant evergreen shrub up to 6 ft. high. Leaves yellow-green, ½ in. long and arranged on the twigs in six vertical rows. This is a conspicuous feature when viewed from directly above the apical end of twig. Flowers are borne in the axils of the upper leaves and have 2 very small petals and 2 short stamens. Fruit 2-seeded. Due perhaps to the adaptation of this species to a particular and forbidding habitat frequent attempts at cultivation have been unsuccessful.

Old fields and scrub oak woods in the dry sterile sandy regions. Summer.

The range formerly is recorded as from Nova Scotia to Florida, but it is not now known north of South Carolina.

LEATHERWOOD: *Dirca palustris* Linnaeus.

A deciduous shrub to 6 ft. tall with obovate leaves and small, pale yellow flowers arising 2 or 3 together from leaf axils, before the leaves. Fruit red, fleshy and 1-seeded.

Rich woods, mostly Piedmont. Spring. Quebec to Florida.

THREE-SEEDED MERCURY: *Acalypha rhombifolia* Rafinesque.

A branching, somewhat pubescent annual to 30 in. tall. Leaves ovate, shallowly toothed, to 3 in. long and with petiole. Flowers surrounded and partly hidden by toothed, leaflike bracts in the leaf axils. Petals none. Fruit a capsule.

Woods, fields and margins, throughout. Summer. Quebec to Florida.

Piriqueta caroliniana (Walter) Urban is a perennial herb to 15 in. high tending to form small colonies from root sprouts. Stem densely pubescent; leaves alternate, oblong, sessile or nearly so and pubescent beneath; flowers orange-yellow, about 1 in. wide and 5 parted; fruit a capsule.

Sandy margins, Coastal Plain. Summer. South Carolina to Florida.

SMOOTH SUMAC: *Rhus glabra* Linnaeus.

Usually a sparsely branched perennial shrub but occasionally attaining a diameter of 4 in. and a height of 20 ft. Leaves odd-pinnate with 9–25 lanceolate leaflets with toothed margins, pointed tips and whitened undersurfaces. Flowers very small, greenish-white and in dense panicles. Corolla lobes 5; stamens 5. Fruit bright red and covered with minute hairs. Leaves show good autumn colors.

Common in open upland sites. Summer. New England to Florida.

WINGED SUMAC: *R. copallina* Linnaeus.

Similar but somewhat smaller with the obvious difference that the leaf-rachis is winged throughout.

STAGHORN SUMAC: *R. typhina* Linnaeus.

Resembles *R. glabra* except that the stems are covered with a coarse pubescence. Mountains.

LEATHERWOOD, TI-TI: *Cyrilla racemiflora* Linnaeus.

Freely branched shrub or small tree up to 20 ft. tall. Leaves 2–4 in. long, semievergreen, glabrous, oblanceolate and entire. Flowers white, very small and borne in many-flowered racemes. Petals 5, alternating with the stamens. Fruit a very small capsule ripening a bright yellow.

Swamps and stream banks, mostly in the Coastal Plain. Early summer. Virginia to Florida.

WINTERBERRY: *Ilex laevigata* (Pursh) Gray.

Deciduous shrub to 8 ft. tall. Leaves elliptic to broader, 2–4 in. long, finely toothed, and hairy on the veins beneath. Flowers small, axillary, greenish and 5- to 7-parted. Some plants produce staminate flowers only; others only pistillate. Berries ¼ in. long and red.

Swamps, pocosins and wet margins. Coastal Plain.

Other similar species are the wide ranging *I. verticillata* (Linnaeus) Gray with glabrous sepals, and *I. ambigua* (Michaux) Torrey with flower parts in fours. *I. decidua* Walter has much smaller leaves and berries.

STRAWBERRY BUSH, HEARTS-BURSTING-WITH-LOVE:
Euonymus americanus Linnaeus.

Slender erect shrub to 5 ft. tall with green bark. Leaves thickish but deciduous, elliptic, 1½–3 in. long, toothed and almost sessile. Flowers solitary or few together, greenish-purple, ½ in. wide and with parts in fives. Fruit a 3- to 5-lobed, warty, crimson capsule which splits open at maturity revealing red-coated seeds.

Moist woods. Early summer. New York to Florida.

E. atropurpureus Jacquin is a shrub or small tree with larger leaves, flower parts in 4s and a smooth capsule. Rare, low forests and along stream banks, mostly Piedmont. Virginia to Georgia.

BLADDERNUT: *Staphylea trifoliata* Linnaeus.

A slender deciduous shrub with trifoliate leaves that are finely toothed around the margins. Flowers are produced along with the leaves in small hanging clusters. Fruit is a greatly inflated 1½ in. long thin-walled capsule.

Low woods and wet margins. Massachusetts to Quebec and south to Florida.

DWARF BUCKEYE: *Aesculus pavia* Linnaeus.

Deciduous shrub or small tree from enlarged root. Leaves palmately compound with 5 lanceolate toothed leaflets. Flowers somewhat tubular, red or yellowish and in terminal racemes. Fruit globose with a leathery covering which at maturity splits into 3 parts revealing 1 or 2 large chestnut-brown seeds, vaguely resembling "buck eyes."

Rich moist woods, Piedmont and Coastal Plain. Spring. Virginia to Florida.

A. sylvatica Bartram is similar but has greenish flowers tinged with cream or pink.

TOUCH-ME-NOT, JEWELWEED, BALSAM: *Impatiens biflora* Walter.

Glabrous annual to 4 ft. in height. Leaves pale green, somewhat watery in appearance, alternate, ovate, 1–4 in. long and shallowy toothed. Flowers 1 in. long, spurred, in small axillary racemes and drooping on slender pedicels. Corolla orange-yellow with darker spots. Capsules green, spindle-shaped, ¾ in. long and at maturity bursting readily when touched, whence the Latin name and popular apellation.

Open stream margins and springy places. Summer. Newfoundland to South Carolina

I. pallida Nuttall is the mountain form with yellow to cream flowers.

NEW JERSEY TEA: *Ceanothus americanus* Linnaeus.

A low deciduous shrub with ovate 3-ribbed toothed leaves. Flowers cream to white and in terminal clusters. Fruit 3-lobed and dry.

Dry or rocky woods. Early summer. Maine to Florida.

During the American Revolution leaves of this plant were considered one of the best substitutes for tea.

INDIAN CHERRY: *Rhamnus caroliniana* Walter.

Small deciduous tree to 25 ft. high. Leaves oblong to elliptic, 2–4 in. long, dark green with prominent veins and obscurely toothed. Flowers very small, axillary and with parts in fives. Fruit black at maturity, 3-seeded and about ⅓ in. long.

Rich woods and bluffs. Early summer. Virginia to Florida.

SAGERETIA: *Sageretia minutiflora* (Michaux) Trelease.

One of the rarest shrubs, in need of recognition and cultivation. In garden or yard it is something to be proud of and to talk about. May grow to 8 ft. tall and has many short pubescent, pointed branches. The leaves, to 1 in. long, are opposite, deciduous, glabrous and barely toothed. Flowers are very small sessile, crowded and 5-parted. Fruits are purplish black, ¼ in. long, 1- to 4-seeded and long persistent on stem.

Sand, dunes and shell mounds, coastal. Late summer. Charleston southward into Georgia.

SILKY CAMELLIA: *Stewartia malachodendron* Linnaeus.

Deciduous shrub or small tree up to 15 ft. tall. Leaves 1½–3 in. long, broadly elliptic, obscurely toothed and pubescent beneath. Flowers axillary and 2–3 in. wide. Petals 5, white. Stamens numerous, filaments purple. Fruit a broad capsule ½ in. long. Seeds wingless.

Low woods, Coastal Plain. Late spring. Virginia to Florida.

MOUNTAIN CAMELLIA: *S. ovata* (Cavanilles) Weatherby.

Plant has broader, ovate leaves with long pointed tips.

71

ST. PETER'S-WORT: *Ascyrum stans* Michaux.

Low shrub with erect, branched stem 1–2 ft. high. Leaves firm, oblong, ½–1½ in. long and rounded at tip. Flowers yellow, showy, 1 in. or more in width. Stamens numerous. Fruit a small capsule.

Moist, sandy margins, Piedmont and Coastal Plain. Summer. New Jersey to Florida.

ST. ANDREW'S CROSS: *A. hypericoides* Linnaeus.

Shrub is smaller and more generally distributed. Summer.

HYPERICUM: *Hypericum denticulatum* Walter.

A variable, erect herbaceous species to 1½ ft. tall. Stem 4-angled. Leaves opposite and to 1 in. long. Flowers several, yellow and borne in flat-topped cluster. Stamens many. Fruit a capsule.

Balds, wet margins, ditches and open pinelands. Summer. New Jersey to Florida.

Other herbaceous species are *H. punctatum* Lambert with conspicuously dark-dotted leaves and *H. gentianoides* (Linnaeus) BSP., sometimes referred to as pineweed, povertygrass or orangegrass, has leaves as minute appressed scales. Old fields, margins and rock outcrops, throughout. Summer. New England to Florida.

ST.-JOHN'S-WORT: *Hypericum frondosum* Michaux.

Branching semievergreen shrub about 3 ft. tall. Bark exfoliating in thin layers. Leaves opposite, narrowly oblong, 1–1½ in. long, dark shining green. Flowers showy, bright yellow and about 1¼ in. wide. Petals 5; stamens numerous. Fruit a capsule. Often in cultivation.

Rocky woods, mostly in the mountains. Summer. North Carolina to Georgia.

Other similar species, but with flowers less than 1 in. wide, are *H. prolificum* Linnaeus with capsules more than ¼ in. long and *H. densiflorum* Pursh with capsules less than ¼ in. long. Both wide ranging.

SANDHILL HYPERICUM: *Hypericum lloydii* (Svenson) P. Adams.

Low-growing matted shrub has very narrow linear leaves to 1 in. long that are semievergreen, and a profusion of bright yellow flowers. Capsules very small and 3-celled.

Dry, sandy, open woods, from the lower Piedmont into the upper Coastal Plain. Summer. North Carolina to Florida.

BLUE VIOLET: *Viola papilionacea* Pursh.

A stemless plant with leaves and flowers arising from underground rhizome. Leaves cordate to reniform, 1–2 in. across. Fruit a capsule. Seeds dark brown.

Low woods and clearings. Spring. Massachusetts to Georgia.

Other widely distributed blue violets from underground stems are *V. affinis* Le Conte with narrowly pointed cordate leaves, and two with leaves deeply lobed for half their length or more: *V. pedata* Linnaeus (Bird-Foot Violet) with none of the petals bearded and *V. palmata* Linnaeus with one or more of the petals bearded.

WHITE VIOLET: *V. primulifolia* Linnaeus.

Leaves lanceolate or broader, shallowly toothed and abruptly narrowed to a winged petiole, arise from a slender rhizome. Flowers equaling or taller than the leaves. Petals beardless and with brown or purplish lines on lower three petals.

Wet margins, throughout. Spring. New England to Florida.

V. lanceolate Linnaeus is similar to preceding but has very narrowly lanceolate leaves that are gradually narrowed into a winged petiole.

Wet sandy margins, Coastal Plain. Spring. New England to Florida.

JOHNNY-JUMP-UP: *V. rafinesquii* Greene.

A winter annual of fields and roadsides. New York to Georgia. Also, the similar and closely related European introduction *V. arvensis* Murray with wintergreen scented roots.

PANSY: *V. tricolor* Linnaeus.

Also an introduction from the Old World. It is widespread.

YELLOW VIOLET: *Viola hastata* Michaux.

Stem 3–7 in. tall from white fleshy rhizome. Leaves 2–4 near summit of stem, long heart-shaped and to 2½ in. in length, toothed and often mottled green. Flowers bright yellow and on slender stalks. Central petal with purple lines. Fruit a capsule.

Rich woods. Spring. Pennsylvania to Florida.

Other yellow violets are *V. tripartita* Elliott, an erect type with deeply divided leaves of the Piedmont and mountains, and *V. rotundifolia* Michaux without an above ground stem and restricted to mountain coves.

GREEN VIOLET; *Hybanthus concolor* (Forster) Sprengel.

An erect, pubescent perennial to 2 ft. tall with long-pointed elliptic leaves. Flowers small, greenish, from the leaf axils and commonly in pairs hanging from slender, jointed pedicels. Fruit a capsule.

Rich woods, Piedmont and upper Coastal Plain. Spring. Ontario to Georgia.

ROCKROSE: *Helianthemum canadense* (Linnaeus) Michaux.

A small shrubby, pubescent, little branched perennial from rhizomes. Leaves narrow and to 1 in. long. Flowers yellow, to 1 in. wide and with 5 petals. Late flowers have no petals. Fruit a capsule.

Dry, sandy, open sites, mainly Coastal Plain. Summer. Maine to Georgia.

TAMARISK, SALT CEDAR, FIRE CEDAR; *Tamarix gallica* Linnaeus.

An introduced mostly evergreen shrub or small tree with slender, flexuous branches with very small, almost scalelike, alternate, sessile, gray-green leaves. Flowers are borne in long, slender, crowded axillary racemes, are 5-parted and white or pinkish in color. Fruits are capsular and seeds have soft hairs attached.

Escaped to sandy and waste places, mostly coastal. Late spring and summer. Virginia to Florida.

PRICKLY PEAR, CACTUS: *Opuntia compressa* (Salisbury) Macbride.

Fleshy and thickened perennial. Stems green, usually spiny, prostrate or spreading, conspicuously jointed and the joints greatly compressed. Leaves missing or present only briefly in the spring as small fleshy structures. Flowers bright yellow, 2–3 in. wide. Stamens numerous. Fruit 1–1½ in. long, purplish-red and edible except for minute spines likely to be on the surface.

Exposed, dry sandy situations. Early summer. Massachusetts to Georgia. *O. vulgare* Miller is similar but much larger and frequently cultivated.

O. drummondii Graham has small, short, little compressed segments and very long spines. Sandy soil, Coastal Plain. Summer.

MAYPOP: *Passiflora incarnata* Linnaeus.

A trailing plant with deeply 3-lobed leaves, 2 in. wide blue flowers with prominent fringe and large yellowish, edible fruits.

Thickets and margins, throughout. Summer. Virginia to Florida and west.

LITTLE MAYPOP: *P. lutea* Linnaeus.

High climbing with shallowly 3-lobed leaves, ¾ in. wide yellowish flowers and ½ in. long black fruits. Both maypops have tendrils.

Woods and thickets, throughout. Spring and summer. Pennsylvania to Florida.

ROSE MALLOW: *Hibiscus moscheutos* Linnaeus.

A robust, closely pubescent perennial to 6 ft. high with ovate, toothed, petioled leaves to 8 in. long. Flowers to 6 in. wide, 5-parted, white or cream with red or purple centers. Fruit 1 in. long, 5-celled capsule.

Swamps, marshes and other wet open places, throughout. Summer. Maryland to Florida and west.

MEADOW BEAUTY: *Rhexia alifanus* Walter.

Upright unbranched perennial herb to 3 ft. tall. Leaves pointing up the stem, 1–2½ in. long, opposite, lanceolate and long pointed with midvein conspicuously lacking in chlorophyll and appearing whitish. Flowers about 1½ in. in diameter and borne terminally. Petals four, pinkish-purple and falling usually by noon. Stamens 8. Fruit an urn-shaped capsule, locally of interest in dried arrangements. This is the largest of the several species of *Rhexia* that occur in the Southeast.

Low open woods and roadsides of the Coastal Plain. Late spring. North Carolina to Florida.

The following differ in that their stems are beset with stiff brownish hairs. In *R. mariana* the stem is not winged and the stem faces are unequal. *R. virginica* has a winged stem and the stem faces are about equal. Both are Linnaean species, have pinkish-purple to white flowers and are widespread.

WAXWEED: *Cuphea carthagensis* (Jacquin) Macbride.

Coarsely pubescent annual with entire elliptic leaves and small purplish flowers with 6 narrow petals extending from a cylindrical calyx tube, which at maturity splits open, exposing yellowish seeds.

Marshes and ditches, Coastal Plain. Summer. New Hampshire to Georgia.

PRIMROSE WILLOW: *Ludwigia decurrens* Harper.

An erect herb with 4-angled, or 4-winged stem, lanceolate leaves to 4 in. long and on very short petioles and yellow flowers, usually of 4 petals fragilely attached. Capsule short and 4-sided.

Wet margins and banks, throughout. Summer. Virginia to Florida.

Jussiaea uruguayensis (Cambessedes) Hara is a related plant introduced from South America with hairy stems and leaves, leaves to 5 in. long; flowers yellow and 1½ in. wide; capsule cylindric and 1 in. or more long.

Shallow waters where it tends to form floating mats. Summer. New York into South America.

HERCULES'-CLUB: *Aralia spinosa* Linnaeus.

Upright and little branched deciduous shrub or small tree up to 20 ft. high. Stem and leaves coarsely prickly. Leaves up to 3 ft. long, twice or thrice compound; leaflets 1–3 in. long, ovate and serrate. Flowers small, greenish-white and purple berries about ⅕ in. in diameter.

Rich woods and stream banks. Summer. Delaware to Florida.

HERCULES'-CLUB, PRICKLY ASH, *Zanthoxylum clava-herculis* Linnaeus.

Also a small, very spiny tree. Leaves pinnate, leaflets 5–15. Flowers and fruits small and numerous. Maritime forests and dunes. Virginia to Florida.

This is sometimes referred to as "Toothache" tree in allusion to the hot, racy pungence given off by the leaves that perhaps makes one forget the toothache.

QUEEN ANNE'S LACE, WILD CARROT: *Daucus carota* Linnaeus.

Rough-hairy branched biennial to 3 ft. high from stout tap root. Leaves alternate and much dissected; leaf segments about ¹⁄₁₆–⅛ in. wide. Flowers white, small, very numerous and arranged in umbrella-shaped clusters. With the maturation of the fruits and flower clusters become bird's nest-shaped. Fruit very small, bristly and in pairs.

Dry fields and waste places. Early summer. Quebec to Florida.

This is an introduction from Southern Europe and North Africa. The cultivated Carrot is the variety *sativa* De Candolle.

78

BUTTON SNAKEROOT: *Eryngium yuccifolium* Michaux.

Stiffly erect, coarse, perennial herb up to 3 ft. high. Leaves 6–24 in. long, linear or nearly so, of a tough leathery texture and usually with slender spines along the margin. Inflorescence of greenish-white, many-flowered, ovoid heads ¾ in. long. Petals inconspicuous. Fruit small. Dry open woods and roadsides. Summer. New Jersey to Florida.

In contrast to the above *E. prostratum* Nuttall is a small, slender, prostrate perennial with thin ovate or narrower leaves, some toothed or deeply lobed. Tiny blue flowers are in small cylindric heads.

Wet sandy ditches and low margins, Piedmont and Coastal Plain. Summer. Virginia to Florida and west.

PENNYWORT: *Hydrocotyle umbellata* Linnaeus.

A glabrous, creeping, semievergreen perennial herb with circular, shallowly notched leaves to 2 in. wide, to the center of which a long petiole is attached. Flowers small, greenish and clustered at top of stalk as tall or taller than the leaves. Fruit a 2-seeded structure.

Low, open areas, mostly Coastal Plain. Spring and summer. Nova Scotia to Florida.

SUNDROPS: *Oenothera fruticosa* Linnaeus.

An erect perennial to 2 ft. high with lanceolate, pubescent leaves to 3 in. long. Petioles short or none. Flowers yellow and 1½ in. wide, petals 4, capsule club-shaped.

Dry margins, throughout. Summer. Nova Scotia to Florida.

O. speciosa Nuttall has pink flowers to 2½ in. wide. This is native to the prairies and cultivated and sometimes escaped here.

O. laciniata Hill is a weedy species with irregularly lobed leaves and 1 in. wide yellow flowers.

Fields and roadsides, throughout. Summer and fall.

EVENING PRIMROSE: *O. biennis* Linnaeus.

An erect form to 4 ft. tall with lanceolate or wider leaves irregularly lobed. Flowers several and terminal, yellow, 2 in. wide with long calyx tube.

Weedy, moist margins, throughout. Summer. Canada to Florida.

FLOWERING DOGWOOD: *Cornus florida* Linnaeus.

Widely branched small tree to 25 ft. high. Twigs usually greenish. Leaves 2½–4 in. long, ovate, not toothed, dark green above and pale beneath. Flowers appearing before the leaves, small, yellowish and in head-like clusters, conspicuously surrounded by 4 large white or pink petaloid bracts. Fruit about ½ in. long, red and containing 1–2 stony seeds. The generic name *Cornus,* meaning horn, alludes to the hardness of the wood. An earlier common name, dagwood, comes from the Old English word for dagger. State flower of North Carolina and Virginia.

Woodlands. Early spring. Maine to Florida.

SWAMP DOGWOOD, RED WILLOW: *C. stricta* Lamarck.

A medium-sized shrub with red twigs and stems. Flowers small, white and in corymbs. Fruit blue.

C. amomum Miller, differs in that second year stems have brown pith instead of white.

ALTERNATE-LEAVED DOGWOOD: *C. alternifolia* Linnaeus, f.

Shrub or small tree with alternate leaves and clusters of small flowers maturing to blue berries.

Woodlands, mountains and upper Piedmont. Spring. Nova Scotia to Georgia.

GALAX: *Galax aphylla* Linnaeus.

Perennial evergreen herb with flowering stem to 2 ft. high. Leaves more or less orbicular with deeply cordate bases, toothed margins, shiny surfaces and long petioles extending down to matted underground stems. Flowers small, white and deeply 5-lobed. Fruit a small 3-celled capsule.

Rich moist woods, mostly in the mountains. Summer. Virginia to Georgia.

OCONEE-BELLS, JACKSCREW-ROOT: *Shortia galacifolia* Torrey and Gray.

Perennial evergreen spreading by short runners to form colonies. Leaves broad, rounded at the apex, bluntly toothed, shiny green and often purple tinged, with very prominent veins and long petioles. Flowers white, about 1 in. across and borne separately on stalks about as long as the petioles. Petals 5, separate and toothed at apex.

On wooded banks of mountain streams in a few little-frequented areas. Spring. North and South Carolina.

Inadequately reported early in U.S. history from a remote mountain area, it was not rediscovered for over a century. Though once greatly restricted in its distribution it is now widespread through transplanting.

SWEET PEPPER BUSH, WHITE ALDER: *Clethra alnifolia* Linnaeus.

Deciduous shrub up to 6 ft. high often forming small colonies from underground stems. Leaves 2–4 in. long, obovate and finely toothed. Flowers 5-parted, white, ⅓ in. wide and closely borne on 3–5 in. long terminal racemes. Fruit a very small capsule.

Swamps, margins and moist woods, most abundant in the Coastal Plain. Summer. Maine to Florida.

C. acuminata Michaux is the mountain form and has larger and more pointed leaves. Rich woods. Summer. Pennsylvania to Georgia.

DOG LAUREL: *Leucothoe axillaris* (Lamarck) D. Don.

This evergreen shrub has arching stems to 4 ft. high bearing 2-ranked alternate, finely toothed long pointed leaves to 5 in. Long and waxy white tubular flowers in dense terminal racemes.

Stream banks and wet woods, throughout. Spring. Virginia to Florida.

MOUNTAIN FETTERBUSH, MOUNTAIN ANDROMEDA: *Pieris floribunda* (Pursh) Bentham and Hooker.

Evergreen shrub with elliptic leaves to 2 in. long. Flowers tubular, waxy white, ¼ in. long and in small, branched terminal arrangement.

Rich woods, mountains. Spring. Virginia to Georgia.

LEATHERLEAF: *Cassandra calyculata* (Linnaeus) D. Don.

Evergreen shrub to 4 ft. high with alternate, entire, elliptic leaves to 2 in. long. Small, tubular, whitish flowers are borne in terminal racemes with each small flower subtended by a half-size leaf.

Pocosins and bays, Coastal Plain. Spring. Labrador to South Carolina.

PIPSISSEWA, RAT'S-BANE: *Chimaphila maculata* (Linnaeus) Pursh.

Small shrub with 1–4 lanceolate, sharply toothed stem leaves that are white along the veins. Flowers few, 5 petals, white. Dry to moist woods, throughout. Spring. Massachusetts to Georgia.

SHINLEAF: *Pyrola rotundifolia* (Sweet) Fernald.

Small shrub with 1–6 circular basal leaves. Flowers white, petals separate. Upland woods, mountains and Piedmont. Summer. Nova Scotia to North Carolina.

WINTERGREEN, CHECKERBERRY: *Gaulthera procumbens* Linnaeus.

A shrub to 8 in. high, frequently branched and with several stem leaves. Entire plant is aromatic and a commercial source of wintergreen. Flowers white to pinkish tubular; fruit a berry. In scattered woodland locations, throughout. Summer. Newfoundland to North Carolina.

TRAILING ARBUTUS: *Epigaea repens* Linnaeus.

A trailing shrub with stems to 1½ ft. long, ovate leaves and white to pink, very fragrant flowers spreading corolla lobes. Sandy or rocky woods, throughout. Spring. Newfoundland to Florida.

LAMB-KILL, WICKY: *Kalmia angustifolia* var. *caroliniana* (Small) Fernald.

A smaller shrub with pale green usually opposite leaves which are finely pubescent beneath. Flowers smaller and in lateral clusters.

Sandy woods and moist margins. Late spring. Maritime Provinces to South Carolina.

K. hirsuta Walter. Similar to above but with calyx conspicuously pubescent. Limited to the Coastal Plain.

MOUNTAIN LAUREL, IVY: *Kalmia latifolia* Linnaeus.

Medium-sized shrub, much branched from the base, forming a rounded top. Leaves alternate, evergreen, coriaceous, 2–4 in. long, dark green above, lighter beneath and smooth with entire margins. Flowers ¾ in. across in terminal clusters, white to rose-colored with purple markings within. The somewhat bowl-shaped corolla is shallowly 5-lobed and has 10 pockets in which the individual stamens are held under tension. Normally, release from the pockets is occasioned by the touch of an insect visitor whereupon the stamen snaps toward the center showering forth pollen. This species transplants very easily if at the time the entire top is removed about 6 in. above ground level.

In mountain areas "breaking ivy" has long been a practice. Branch tips are snapped off in quantity, sold by the pound and shipped to northeastern markets for Christmas greenery.

Dry, rocky slopes and high stream banks particularly in the mountains but extends along river bluffs to near the coast. Late spring. New Brunswick to Florida.

SAND MYRTLE: *Leiophyllum buxifolium* (Bergius) Elliott.

A low shrub seldom over 3 ft. high and much branched toward the summit. The very small elliptic evergreen leaves are leathery and numerous toward the branch tip. This gives to the plant a rather boxwood-like appearance. Flowers white or pinkish, about ⅓ in. across and borne in clusters from the axils of the upper leaves. Petals 5 and separate. Stamens 10, the filaments often red or purplish. Fruit a small capsule. Where found it often grows abundantly and in bloom presents a showy display. Transplanting unknown.

Occurs mainly in sandy areas of the Coastal Plain and on mountain bluffs and summits. Spring. New Jersey to South Carolina.

SHOOTING STAR: *Dodecatheon meadia* Linnaeus.

Perennial from thick roots with entire, narrowly oblanceolate leaves to 8 in. long in a basal rosette. Flower stalk to 18 in. high with 3–9 nodding, white flowers at top. Petals 5, to 1 in. long and pointing backward; stamens protruding forward. Fruit a capsule.

Rich, moist woods, mountains and Piedmont. Spring. District of Columbia to Georgia.

WATER PIMPERNEL: *Samolus parviflorus* Rafinesque.

A rather succulent plant from a basal rosette of oblanceolate leaves to 3 in. long; stem leaves alternate and smaller. Stem branched and with terminal racemes of small white, 5-parted flowers. Fruit a capsule.

Wet, often shady places, lower Piedmont and Coastal Plain. Summer. Canada to Florida.

SEA LAVENDER: *Limonium carolinianum* (Walter) Britton.

Fleshy perennial from a basal rosette of oblanceolate leaves with rounded tips. Flower stalk is well raised and much branched. Flowers are numerous, about ¼ in. wide, lavender and 5-parted. Fruit 1-seeded.

Brackish marshes. Late summer. New York to Florida.

FETTERBUSH: *Lyonia lucida* (Lamarck) K. Koch.

Medium-sized, distinctly evergreen shrub with smooth green branches showing three low angles or wings. Leaves elliptic. 1½–3 in. long, thick, entire, rather light green and bordered all around with a nearly marginal vein. Flowers white or pinkish, in small clusters from the upper leaf. Corolla ⅓ in. long, tubular and with 5 short lobes. Capsule subglobose.

Low woods and thickets of the Coastal Plain. Late spring. Virginia to Florida.

STAGGERBUSH: *L. mariana* (Linnaeus) D. Don.

Deciduous shrub seldom over 3 ft. high. Leaves elliptic to oblong, 1–2½ in. long, entire and glabrous except for the nerves beneath. Flowers white or pinkish in pendant clusters from the axils of the leaves, each suspended by a pedicel as long or longer than the corolla. Corolla tubular, ½ in. long and shallowly 5-lobed. Capsule abruptly narrowed toward the apex.

Dry or wet woods and borders. Lower Piedmont and Coastal Plain. Early summer. Rhode Island to Florida.

MALEBERRY: *L. ligustrina* (Linnaeus) De Candolle.

Deciduous shrub with ½–1½ in. long leaves and short white globose corollas abruptly narrowed at apex. The small globose, berrylike capsule has resulted in the idea that this is a male type blueberry!

Occasional throughout from Maine to Florida.

FETTERBUSH: *Eubotrys recurva* (Buckley) Britton.

Deciduous shrub with small tubular white or pinkish flowers in leafless terminal racemes that show before or with leaves; winged seeds.

Bogs and wet woods, mountains and upper Piedmont.

E. racemosa (Linnaeus) Nuttall is a related deciduous shrub also with small tubular white or pinkish flowers in leafless terminal racemes showing before or with leaves.

Pocosins and wet woods, Coastal Plain and lower Piedmont.

INDIAN PIPE: *Monotropa uniflora* Linnaeus.

Non-green, fleshy herb, waxy white or pinkish in color and not over 6 in. tall. Leaves scalelike and of the same color as the stem. Flower solitary, nodding and odorless. Petals 4 or 5; stamens twice as many as the petals. Fruit an erect capsule containing many very fine seeds.

Plant grows parasitically on the roots of deciduous trees or soil fungi. Summer. Newfoundland to Florida.

M. hypopithys Linnaeus is smaller but has several flowers per stem. Stem pubescent.

The closely related *Monotropsis odorata* Schweinitz is small brownish-yellow, red or purplish with a smooth stem and several small flowers at tip. Fruit a berry instead of a capsule as above. Hard to find.

BEECHDROPS: *Epifagus virginiana* (Linnaeus) Barton.

A branching, pale brown or purplish plant to 15 in. high with scalelike alternate leaves and solitary axillary flowers, purplish and ½ in. long.

Parasitic on the roots of beech, throughout. Late summer. Nova Scotia to Florida.

ONE-FLOWERED CANCER ROOT: *Orobanche uniflora* Linnaeus.

An unbranched pale bluish plant to 5 in. tall from a swolen base surrounded by overlapping leaf scales. Flower pubescent, violet and almost 1 in. long.

Parasitic, perhaps on the roots of several species of hardwoods. Rich woods, mostly mountains and Piedmont. Summer. Newfoundland to Florida.

BARTONIA: *Bartonia virginica* (Linnaeus) Britton, Sterns and Poggenburg.

Erect, slender, unbranched purplish or yellowish plants with mostly opposite scalelike leaves and a terminal arrangement of 2–6 small, 4-lobed, purplish flowers. Entire plant to 18 in. high. Fruit a capsule.

Marshes, bays, savannahs and open, wet places. Summer and early fall. Quebec to Florida.

SOURWOOD: *Oxydendrum arboreum* (Linnaeus) De Candolle.

Small deciduous, gray-barked tree, seldom erect but growing upward in a leaning or inclined position. Leaves 3–5 in. long, elliptic, finely toothed and tapering at the apex, turning scarlet in the fall. Flowers small, numerous and borne on several 1-sided racemes clustered at the tips of the branches. Corollas white, tubular and 5-lobed. Flowers highly regarded by beekeepers as a source of mild, clear honey.

Sometimes sold as an ornamental with the name "Lily-of-the-Valley Tree" or because the leaves develop nice autumn colors.

Woods. Summer. Pennsylvania to Florida.

PERSIMMON: *Diospyros virginiana.* Linnaeus.

Deciduous tree with checkered bark and alternate entire leaves to 4 in. long. Flowers staminate or perfect, fragrant, yellowish and about ¼ in. long. Fruit a large edible berry.

Dry or wet woods and margins, throughout. New York to Florida.

COMMON PRIVET: *Ligustrum sinense* Loureiro.

Asian introduction; tall shrub or small tree, semievergreen with elliptic leaves to 2 in. long and pubescent on the veins beneath. Small white, fragrant, 4-parted flowers are borne in many-flowered terminal panicles, followed by small, bluish, 1-seeded berries.

Low woods and waste places, throughout. Late spring. Widespread.

LARGE-LEAVED PRIVET: *L. japonicum* Thunberg.

Larger, darker, almost glossy-green leaves and glabrous twigs. More scattered and southern in its distribution.

POLYPREMUM: *Polypremum procumbens* Linnaeus.

Low, glabrous perennial branching out from a central crown. Leaves opposite, linear and about ½ in. long. Flowers are axillary, white, 4-parted and ¼ in. long, or less. Fruit is a capsule.

Open, dry woods, margins and old fields, Piedmont and Coastal Plain. Summer. Delaware to Florida.

HOARY PINK AZALEA: *Rhododendron canescens* (Michaux) Sweet.

Deciduous shrub whose leaves, particularly the young ones, are whitened with a gray or hoary pubescence. The leaves appear before the flowers and the corolla lobes are shorter than the tube.

Swamps and moist woods of the Coastal Plain. Spring. Delaware to Florida.

Several other deciduous species with flowers ranging from white to purple occur:

R. atlanticum (Ashe) Rehder is a dwarf, mostly white, colony former that ranges the Coastal Plain from Virginia south.

R. viscosum (Linnaeus) Torrey is a tall, mostly white type occurring throughout from Maine to Florida.

FLAME AZALEA: *Rhododendron calendulaceum* (Michaux) Torrey.

Deciduous shrub seldom over 4 ft. high. Leaves elliptic, 2–3 in. long and only about half grown at flowering time. Flowers in terminal clusters and from pale to orange-yellow. Corollas about 2 in. across. Stamens 5 and long exerted. Because of its ornamental value this species has been much sought-after by those who sell wild plants.

Mountain woods. Late spring. Pennsylvania to Georgia.

PINK HONEYSUCKLE, PINK AZALEA: *Rhododendron nudiflorum* Torrey.

Deciduous shrub to 6 ft. tall. Leaves 2–3 in. long, oblanceolate and only beginning to appear at flowering time. Flowers pink and borne in terminal clusters. Corolla 1½ in. across, pubescent and with the lobes longer than the tube. This is a hardy wild flower and deserves more horticultural attention than it has received.

Woods and swamps. Spring. Vermont to South Carolina.

SMOOTH AZALEA: *R. arborescens* (Pursh) Torrey.

Similar to *R. viscosum* differing mainly in having glabrous, smooth, young twigs and being restricted to the mountains, and mostly the upper Piedmont. Spring. Pennsylvania to Georgia.

MINNIEBUSH: *Menziesia pilosa* (Michaux) Jussieu.

Shrub to 6 ft. high. Leaves deciduous, elliptic, entire, to 3 in. long and hairy in the vein axes beneath. Flowers greenish white to pinkish and 4-lobed. Fruit a capsule.

Balds, high slopes and bogs. Spring. West Virginia to Georgia.

BUTTERFLY BUSH: *Buddleia lindleyana* Fortune.

From China as an ornamental and escaped, this erect, deciduous shrub with arching branches has opposite, lanceolate and long-pointed leaves. Flowers are borne in long terminal racemes; each corolla is tubular but curved, 4-lobed, violet to pinkish and ½ in. long.

Stream banks and waste places, Piedmont and Coastal Plain. Summer. Virginia to Florida. Infrequent.

MOUNTAIN LAUREL: *Rhododendron maximum.* Linnaeus.

Evergreen shrub usually less than 10 ft. high. Leaves thick, oblong, 4–8 in. long, dark green above and paler beneath. Flowers in clusters, white or pinkish and spotted within, with yellow mainly on the upper petal. Corolla about 1½ in. across. Capsule about ½ in. long. State flower of West Virginia.

Rich mountain woods, particularly on bluffs along streams where it forms colonies. Late spring. Virginia to Georgia.

ROSE BAY: *R. catawbiensee* Michaux.

A plant of elevations above 3000 ft. with shorter leaves more whitened beneath and showy pink or purplish flowers.

Bluffs, balds, stream banks and laurel slicks. Late spring. Virginia to Georgia.

IVY: *Rhododendron minus* Michaux.

Straggling evergreen shrub to 8 ft. tall. Leaves 1½–3 in. long, elliptic, dark green above, paler and resinous-dotted beneath. Flowers in clusters, pink to rose and with greenish dots on the upper petal. Corolla deeply 5-lobed and about 1 in. across. Capsule about ½ in. long.

Bluffs and stream banks, mountains and lower Piedmont. Early summer. North Carolina to Georgia.

HIGHBUSH BLUEBERRY: *Vaccinium corymbosum* Linnaeus.

Deciduous shrub to 7 ft. tall. Leaves lanceolate or broader, to 3 in. long and without pubescence except on the veins beneath. Leaves about half grown at flowering time. Flowers white or pinkish, cylindrical, minutely 5-lobed and about ⅓ in. long. Berries blue, sweet and juicy.

Woods. Spring. Nova Scotia to Georgia.

V. atrococcum (Gray) Heller is similar but has wider flowers and downy leaves.

SPARKLEBERRY, WINTER HUCKLEBERRY: *V. arboreum* Marshall.

A semievergreen shrub or small tree to 20 ft. high. Leaves small, elliptic to obovate and entire. Flowers creamy-white, bell-shaped and with very short lobes. Fruit black, mealy and long persisting.

Dry woods throughout except in high mountains. Spring. Virginia to Florida and west.

GOOSEBERRY, DEERBERRY, SQUAW-HUCKLEBERRY: *Polycodium candicans* Small.

A deciduous shrub to 8 ft. high; leaves elliptic to obovate, to 3 in. long and usually whitened, particularly beneath; flowers in leafy racemes with the leaves progressively smaller toward tip, down in some plants to the size of very small bracts; corolla white, bell-shaped and with 5 spreading lobes, growing while maturing; berry green with tint of yellow, pink or purple, to 1 in. in diameter and quite edible on some plants. A possible cultivar.

Dry, mostly sandy woods, generally throughout. Spring. Maine to Georgia.

LOW BLUEBERRY: *Vaccinium vacillans* Torry.

Deciduous shrub to 1½ ft. high often forming small colonies from spreading underground stems. Leaves thickish, usually broadest above the middle, up to 2 in. long and occasionally slightly toothed toward the apex. Flowers appearing with the leaves, white or tinged with red or green, shallowly 5-toothed and about ¼ in. long. Berries blue and sweet. Dry open woods. Spring. Nova Scotia to Georgia.

V. tenellum Aiton is similar but has black berries and is more common in the lower Piedmont and Coastal Plain.

CREEPING BLUEBERRY: *V. crassifolium* Andrews.

A long trailing evergreen with ¼–¾ in. long leaves, few white to pink flowers and black berries.

Pinelands and damp margins of the Coastal Plain. Spring. Virginia to Georgia.

BEAR HUCKLEBERRY: *Gaylussacia dumosa* (Andrzejowski) Torrey and Gray.

Low semievergreen shrub to 15 in. high with leaves to 1 in. long, and commonly widest toward tip and faintly resinous dotted beneath. Flowers cream, cup-shaped and 5-lobed. Berry black.

Dry woods, Coastal Plain and Piedmont. Spring. Newfoundland to Florida.

HONEYCUP: *Zenobia pulverulenta* (Bartram) Pollard.

Deciduous shrub to 8 ft. high. Leaves usually whitened on both sides with a glaucous bloom, somewhat leathery, 1–3 in. long, elliptic and rounded at the ends. Flowers white, fragrant, cup-shaped and about ¼ in. long, borne in unbel-like clusters along a leafless terminal axis. Calyx and corolla 5-lobed; stamens 10. Fruit a depressed capsule.

Damp or wet, sandy woods, bays and pond margins of the Coastal Plain. Early summer. Virginia to South Carolina.

WHORLED LOOSESTRIFE: *Lysimachia quadrifolia* Linnaeus.

An erect little branched perennial with lanceolate or wider leaves in whorls of from 3–6. Flowers yellow with red eye, long pediceled and arising from leaf base. Stolons sometimes present.

Moist to dry margins throughout but more common in upper Piedmont and mountains. Summer. Maine to Georgia.

STORAX: *Styrax americana* Lamarck.

A much branched deciduous shrub to 10 ft. tall. Leaves nearly glabrous, oval to oblong, acute, entire or slightly toothed and from 1–3 in. long. Flowers white, nodding, about ½ in. long and solitary or in 4–5 flowered racemes. Petals 5, white and united at the base only. Stamens 10, style 1.

Stream banks and swamp margins, east of the mountains. Spring. Virginia to Florida.

S. grandiflora Aiton. Smaller shrub than above with obovate leaves which are downy pubescent beneath. Flowers somewhat larger.

Woods, often in dry sandy situations, east of the mountains. Late spring. Virginia to Florida.

SILVER BELL: *Halesia carolina* Linnaeus.

This plant attains only shrub or small tree size in eastern areas but in the Smokies and westward it becomes a large forest tree. On the common small-sized individuals, the bark shows a vertical striping due to the exposure of the lighter-colored inner-bark in the bottom of the fissures. Leaves 3–4 in. long, obovate to elliptic, finely serrate and acuminate at the apex. Flowers in clusters of 2–5, each hanging on a slender pedicel. At the time the young leaves are beginning to appear the white to slightly creamy bell-shaped flowers open but continue to gain in size for a day or two so as to become considerably larger than they were at first. Corolla 4-lobed; stamens 8. Fruit dry, 1–1½ in. long with four very conspicuous longitudinal wings.

Rich, moist woods inland. Spring. Virginia to Florida.

H. diptera Ellis differs in that fruits have only two wings. Southeastern South Carolina and south.

HORSE SUGAR, SWEETLEAF, YELLOWWOOD: *Symplocos tinctoria* (Linnaeus) L'Heritier de Brubelle.

Shrub commonly less than 8 ft. tall. Leaves leathery, dark green above and sometimes tinged with purple, pale and finely pubescent beneath, tardily deciduous, elliptic, 2–4 in. long and obscurely toothed. Leaves sweetish and eaten by livestock. Flowers in sessile clusters of 6–10 on twigs of the previous season. Each flower about ¼ in. in width with 5 petals and numerous long yellowish stamens. Fruit dry, about ⅓ in. long. All parts of this plant were once used as a source of a yellow dye.

Woods and bluffs, most abundant in the Coastal Plain. Flowers appear in early spring before the leaves. Delaware to Florida.

FRINGE TREE: *Chionanthus virginicus* Linnaeus.

Deciduous shrub or occasionally small tree. Leaves entire, oval or narrower and sub-opposite. Flowers in clusters and appearing before or with the leaves. Petals 5 or 6, white, linear and about 1 in. long. Fruit fleshy, purple and ½ in. in length. This species transplants easily and could become a popular ornamental.

Moist woods and borders. Spring. New Jersey to Florida.

YELLOW JESSAMINE: *Gelsemium sempervirens* (Linnaeus) W. T. Aiton.

Evergreen twining vine sometimes climbing to 20 ft. or more. Leaves opposite, lanceolate, 1½–2 in. long and entire. Flowers deep yellow, generally very fragrant and about 1½ in. long. Petals 5 and united to form a conspicuous tube. Fruit a small capsule. State flower of South Carolina.

Common in the Coastal Plain, less abundant in the Piedmont. Spring. Virginia to Florida.

MITERWORT: *Cynoctonum sessilifolium* Walter.

An erect, glabrous annual to 18 in. tall with opposite, entire, sessile leaves rounded at base and to 1 in. long. Stem tip with 2–several short, spreading, slightly recurved branches bearing on their upper surfaces a row of small, crowded, greenish flowers, and later ascending capsules.

Wet, weedy margins, ditches and savannahs, Coastal Plain. Summer. North Carolina to Florida.

PINKROOT, INDIAN PINK, CAROLINA PINK: *Spigelia marilandica* Linnaeus.

Stem 1–2 ft. tall bearing opposite, ovate, pointed leaves from 1–3 in. long. The inflorescence is a one-sided spike of scarlet, tubular flowers from 1½–2 in. long which when fully open show 5 small, widely divergent corolla lobes which are yellow on the inner surface and form a yellow star. Usually only one or two flowers are open at any one time. Fruit a short capsule.

Rich woods. Late spring. Maryland to Florida.

PENNYWORT: *Obolaria virginica* Linnaeus.

Herbaceous and succulent perennial from 2–5 in. high. Leaves opposite, crowded, purplish, widest toward the apex and to ½ in. long. Flowers white or whitish, terminal and also from the axils of the leaves. Corolla about ½ in. long and 4-lobed. Fruit a capsule. Because of its small size and lack of conspicuous coloration this plant is seldom seen.

Rich moist hardwood stands, particularly on bluffs. Early spring. New Jersey to Florida.

SABATIA: *Sabatia difformis* (Linnaeus) Druce.

Tender perennial herb up to 2 ft. tall. Leaves lanceolate or broader, depending on position on the plant, at first in a basal whorl and later opposite on the branched stem. Flowers white and from 1–1½ in. across. Petals narrow, usually 5 and drying yellow. Capsule many seeded.

Moist, sandy woods and margins, mostly on the Coastal Plain. Late summer. North Carolina to Florida.

ROSE PINK: *S. angularis* (Linnaeus) Pursh.

Annual with 4-winged stem, 5 usually pink petals and opposite branches on upper part of stem.

Open woods, old fields and marshes, Summer. throughout.

MARSH PINK: *Sabatia dodecandra* (Linnaeus) Britton, Sterns and Poggenberg.

Slender perennial to 2½ ft. tall. Leaves 1–2 in. long, lanceolate and opposite. Flowers usually pink, about 3 in. broad and terminating slender branches. Corolla with from 8–12 petals overlapping each other toward the base. Capsule ½ in. long.

Marshes near the coast. This plant tolerates salt, brackish or fresh water. Summer. Long Island to Florida.

COLUMBO: *Swertia carolinensis* (Walter) Kuntze.

A tall, smooth, erect herb with rather long, rounded leaves mostly in 4s but vary from 3–9 per whorl. Flowers are borne toward the top of the stem and are about 1 in. wide. The 4 petals are pale with darker streaks. Each petal bears a conspicuous dark-colored gland. Capsule about 1 in. long and somewhat flattened.

Woodlands and margins, Piedmont. Late spring. New York to Georgia.

BLUE STAR: *Amsonia ciliata* Walter.

Perennial herb to 2½ ft. tall usually sending up several stems from one root system. Leaves linear, alternate and numerous. Flowers ½ in. wide, blue and in terminal cluster. Petals 5, united below into a tube. Stamens included within the tube. Fruit a smooth, dry pod 2–5 in. long.

Dry woods and borders, mostly on the Coastal Plain. Late spring. North Carolina to Florida.

INDIAN HEMP: *Apocynum cannabinum* Linnaeus.

Erect, branching, perennial herb with opposite, ovate or narrower, entire leaves. Flowers greenish or white and small. Pods paired, pendant, slender and to 5 in. long.

Roadsides and dry margins, throughout. Early summer. New York to Florida.

BLUE STAR: *Amsonia tabernaemontana* Walter.

Erect, glaberous herb with narrowly lanceolate leaves. The blue flowers give rise to long, slender paired pods opening from the apex allowing the single row of seeds to escape.

Deciduous forests. Late spring. Massachusetts to Georgia.

BUTTERFLY WEED, PLEURISY ROOT, CHIGGER-WEED: *Asclepias tuberosa* Linnaeus.

Perennial to 2 ft. high from deep, branched root. Leaves on the main stem alternate, narrow, 2–3 in. long and pubescent. Flower clusters one-to-several. Flowers yellow to orange-red. Petals 5 and reflexed. The central and most conspicuous part of the flower is known as the corona and is made up of 5 enrolled structures called hoods. Pods 2–4 in. long.

Dry, open woods and clearings. Transplants well. Summer. New Hampshire to Florida.

SAND MILKWEED: *Asclepias humistrata* Walter.

A spreading plant with very broad pink- or white-veined leaves, lavender flowers and a 4- to 6-in. pod.

Open sandy woods and margins of the Coastal Plain. Late spring. North Carolina and south.

A. amplexicaulis Smith is a coarse plant to 2 ft. tall with broad leaves and rose-purple flowers.

Open woods, roadsides and old fields, throughout. Late spring.

VARIEGATED MILKWEED: *Asclepias variegata* Engelmann.

Perennial herb up to 3 ft. tall. Leaves opposite, oblong to ovate, 3 to 5 in. long and abruptly pointed. Flowers in terminal and sometimes axillary clusters. Corollas white and tinged with purple in the center. Petals 5. Hoods globular; horns flattened. Pods erect.

Moist woods and thickets. Spring. New York to Florida.

A. verticillata Linnaeus grows to 2 ft. tall with numerous long narrow leaves, often in verticils, or whorls; greenish flowers sometimes tinged with purple; and smooth, slender pods to 2½ in. long.

Dry sandy or rocky woods, Piedmont and mountains. Summer. New England and south.

SPINEPOD: *Gonolobus carolinensis* (Jacquin) Schultes.

Perennial twining herb with pubescent stem. Leaves heart-shaped, 3–6 in. long, opposite and acutely pointed. Flowers ¾ in. broad, brownish-purple and in axillary clusters. Petals 5 bearing at their point of union a low crown. Pod 4–5 in. long and covered with low spine-like projections.

Moist woods and thickets. Summer. Delaware to Florida.

ANGLEPOD: *G. suberosus* (Linnaeus) Robert Brown.

Similar but for petals that are pubescent on the outside and a pod to 5 in. long that is angled.

Low and swamp forests, mostly Piedmont and Coastal Plain. Summer. Virginia to Alabama.

101

WILD SWEET POTATO VINE, WILD MAN-OF-THE-EARTH:
Ipomoea pandurata (Linnaeus) G. F. W. Meyer.

Perennial trailing or slightly climbing herb from large, deep, tuberlike root. Leaves heart-shaped, from 1½–4 in. long and pubescent on the lower surface. Flowers 2–3 in. long, open-funnel form and white with purple on the inside toward the base. Stamens included within the corolla tube. Fruit a capsule.

Dry woods, margins and thickets. Summer. Connecticut to Florida,

SWEET POTATO: *I. batatas* (Linnaeus) Lamarck.
Widely cultivated as a vegetable.

I. lacunosa Linnaeus is a thinly pubescent climbing annual with heart-shaped or 3-lobed leaves and white flowers.
Fields and margins. Summer. New Jersey to Texas.

COMMON MORNING GLORY:
Ipomoea purpurea (Linnaeus) Roth.

Annual vigorous twining herb with pubescent stem. Leaves broadly heart-shaped or occasionally 3-lobed. Flowers 2–3 in. long, purple, red, bluish or white and borne one to several on slender peduncles arising from the axils of the leaves. Fruit a 4–6 seeded capsule. Introduced from tropical America and often established as a weed.

Roadsides, fields and borders. Summer and early fall. Connecticut to Florida.

I. hederacea (Linnaeus) Jacquin is an introduced pubescent climbing annual with deeply 3-lobed or sometimes only cordate leaves and 1½ in. long light blue flowers.

Fields and margins. Summer. Southeast.

RED MORNING GLORY: *Quamoclit coccinea* (Linnaeus) Moench.

Twining annual to 3 ft. high. Leaves thin and broadly heart-shaped with usually somewhat angular basal lobes. Flowers about 1 in. across, scarlet with pale centers and borne one to several on axillary peduncles longer than the leaves. Fruit a few-seeded capsule. Introduced from tropical America.

Fields, roadsides and waste places. Summer and early fall. Massachusetts to Florida.

CYPRESS VINE: *Q. vulgaris* Chiosy.

Leaves are pinnately divided to the midvein into many very narrow segments. Introduced from tropical America and to limited extent cultivated for ornament. Occasionally escaped to waste places and fields. Summer. Virginia and south.

SAND MORNING GLORY: *Bonamia humistrata* (Walter) Gray.

Small prostrate perennial with alternate, 1–2 in. long elliptic to elliptic-lanceolate leaves and white to pale pinkish flowers to 1 in. wide, commonly borne 3-together. Fruit a capsule.

Dry sandy woods and margins. Coastal Plain and lower Piedmont. Summer. Virginia to Florida.

HEDGE BINDWEED: *Convolvulus sepium* Linnaeus.

Annual twining vine to 6 ft. long with glabrous or pubescent, triangular to arrow-shaped, long-pointed leaves on long petioles. Bracts surrounding lower part of flower heart-shaped and to 1 in. long. Fruit a capsule.

Fields, margins and waste ground, throughout. Summer. Quebec to Florida.

DODDER, LOVE VINE: *Cuscuta campestris* Yuncker.

A rootless, leafless, orange or yellow, annual, parasitic, slender twiner on a variety of herbaceous hosts. Flowers small, white, crowded and shallowly 5-lobed. Fruit a capsule.

Old fields and roadsides, throughout. Summer. Quebec to Florida and west.

MOSS PINK: *Phlox nivalis* Loddiges.

Perennial with persistent, freely branching, prostrate stems forming mats. Leaves opposite, stiffish, persistent, numerous and sharp-pointed. Flowers raised above the mat, 1 in. broad, white or pink with dark eye. Petals 5 and very shallowly toothed. Fruit a small 3-seeded capsule.

Dry or gravelly woods and clearings. Spring. Virginia to Georgia.

P. carolina Linnaeus. Erect perennial to 2½ ft. tall. The stem is usually glabrous. Leaf shape varies from linear to narrowly ovate, all sharp pointed. Calyx about ½ in. long. Corolla pink-purple or occasionally white and to 1 in. wide.

Woods and margins. Late spring and early summer. Maryland and south.

SUMMER PHLOX: *P. paniculata* Linnaeus.

Erect clump-forming perennial to 4 ft. tall. Stem commonly streaked with red. Leaves lanceolate or broader, acuminate and pubescent beneath, Corolla reddish-purple to white, about ¾ in. wide, the tube somewhat pubescent. Much cultivated in several horticultural varieties and frequently escaped.

Rich moist soil. Summer and fall. New York to Georgia.

P. drummondii Hooker is an erect annual commonly branching at base into two or more stems. Leaves opposite, especially below, elliptic and 1–3 in. long. Corolla white to red or variegated and about ½ in. wide.

This is a Western plant that is cultivated and escaped in the Coastal Plain. Spring and summer.

WILD COMFREY: *Cynoglossum virginianum* Linnaeus.

A rough-textured perennial with clasping leaves that are wider toward the tips. The pale blue flowers are followed by bone-white nutlets covered with little hooks.

Rich woods, mostly mountains and Piedmont. Spring. Connecticut to Florida and west.

PUCCOON: *Lithospermum caroliniense* (Walter) MacMillan.

Erect plant from 8–24 in. high from deep perennial root. Leaves alternate, numerous, narrow, 1–2 in. long and rough-hairy. Flowers bright orange-yellow, ¾ in. across and terminal. Early flowers are sterile. Petals 5. Fruit consists of smooth, ivory-white nutlets.

Dry, sandy roadsides and clearings, mostly in the Coastal Plain. Spring and early summer. Virginia to Florida.

CORN GROMWELL: *L. arvense* Linnaeus.

A weedy European annual with narrow, rough-hairy leaves, bluish or white flowers and grayish brown-wrinkled and pitted nutlets.

Fields and roadsides. Late spring. Virginia to Florida and Alabama.

Lithospermum caroliniense

FRENCH MULBERRY, BEAUTYBERRY: *Callicarpa americana* Linnaeus.

Deciduous shrub to 8 ft. high. Leaves ovate, tapering at each end, toothed, and pubescent on both sides in spring. Upper surface may become smooth in summer. Flowers small and in many-flowered clusters in the axils of the upper leaves. Corolla 4–5 lobed and bluish or pinkish in color. Fruit violet-colored. Widey cultivated.

Moist woods and thickets. Summer. Maryland to Florida.

BUCKTHORN: *Bumelia lycioides* (Linnaeus) Persoon.

Semievergreen, often thorny shrub to 6 ft. tall. Leaves 2–3 in. long. elliptic or wider toward tip, alternate but appearing clustered on very short spur twigs. Flowers small, greenish and clustered around leaf bases. Thorns often present around spur twigs. Fruit fleshy and dark.

Swamp woods and bluffs, Piedmont and Coastal Plain. Summer. Virginia to Florida.

WILD OLIVE: *Osmanthus americana* (Linnaeus) Gray.

A small evergreen tree with more or less elliptic leaves to 5 in. long. Flowers small, yellowish and in small axillary clusters. Fruit fleshy, blue and 1-seeded.

Damp forests of the lower Coastal Plain. Spring. Virginia to Florida.

SWAMP PRIVET: *Forestiera acuminata* (Michaux) Poiret.

A rare deciduous shrub or small tree with ovate, entire leaves to 3½ in. long. Flowers are inconspicuous, lacking both sepals and petals and are produced on twig growth of the previous season. Fruits are fleshy, black, elongated, curving and 1-seeded.

Swamp forests, Coastal Plain. Early spring. South Carolina to Georgia.

VERVAIN: *Verbena tenuisecta* Briquet.

Low perennial with decumbent stems and divergent branches. Leaves about as long as wide, triangular in outline and divided into very narrow segments. Flowers almost ½ in. wide, blue, violet or purple and raised on terminal spikes. Petals 5 notched at tips. Introduced from South America.

Roadsides and waste places. Spring and summer. South Carolina to Florida.

V. urticifolia Linnaeus is an erect perennial to 3 ft. in height. The leaves are toothed and broadly lanceolate. The flowers are small, white and remote from one another on inflorescence.

Moist to wet margins, old fields and waste places. Summer and fall. Eastern United States.

Two South American species with 4-angled stems to 6 ft. tall, narrow opposite leaves and tiny purple flowers crowded into dense headlike spikes are *V. bonariensis* Linnaeus and *V. brasiliensis* Vellozo. The former has leaves with clasping bases.

Both are in the Coastal Plain along margins and in waste places.

HELIOTROPE: *Heliotropium amplexicaule* Vahl.

A South American spreading perennial to 1 ft. tall. Leaves alternate, sessile, lanceolate, toothed, pubescent and to 2 in. long. Flowers small, bluish to purplish, 5-lobed and in uncoiling terminal spikes. At a distance easily mistaken for *Verbena tenuisecta*.

Roadsides, fields and waste areas, Piedmont and Coastal Plain. Summer. New Jersey to Florida.

SAMPSON SNAKEROOT, GENTIAN: *Gentiana villosa* Linnaeus.

Erect perennial to 18 in. tall from thick, fleshy roots; leaves sessile or nearly so, elliptic and entire; flowers mostly terminal, sessile, several and crowded, cylindric, scarcely open, 1½ in. long, and greenish or yellowish tinted with purple.

Moist woods, occasional, throughout. Late summer and fall. New Jersey to Florida.

FALSE GROMWELL: *Onosmodium virginianum* (Linnaeus) A. De Candolla.

A rough-hairy, slender-stemmed perennial to 2 ft. high with alternate, broadly lanceolate, strongly veined leaves with little or no petioles. Flowers borne on slender, terminal, recurved branches, each flower partly hidden by a leafy bract. Flowers yellow, almost ½ in. long, 5-lobed and almost equaled in length by the hairy sepals. Style slender and protruding ¼ in. beyond petals. Fruit of 1–4 dull white nutlets.

Dry woods and sandy margins. Piedmont and Coastal Plain. Summer. Maine to Florida.

WILD BERGAMOT: *Monarda fistulosa* Linnaeus.

An erect perennial with narrow, opposite leaves. The terminal head of pink flowers has a whorl of pink or pink-based leaves immediately beneath.

Woods and meadows, more common in the mountains. Summer. New England to Georgia and west.

M. clinopodia Linnaeus is a similar plant with similar range and habitat but with white or pink flowers and bracts of the same color.

BEE-BALM: *Monarda didima* Linnaeus.

An erect perennial with shallowly toothed leaves and an unbranched stem. The terminal head of scarlet flowers has a whorl of red or red-based small leaves immediately beneath.

Rich woods and thickets, upper Piedmont and mountains. Summer. New York to Georgia.

Photo by Mike Creel

DOTTED MONARDA: *Monarda punctata* Linnaeus.

A perennial with simple or branching stem and opposite, lanceolate and somewhat pubescent leaves. The yellow flowers with brown dots are arranged in whorls at the summit of the stem. More conspicuous, however, are the pink, purplish or white leaves borne just below the flowers.

Sandy abandoned fields, thin woodlands and banks, Coastal Plain and into the Piedmont. Late Summer. Long Island to Florida.

NARROW-LEAVED MINT: *Pycnanthemum flexuosum* (Walter) Britton, Sterns and Poggenberg.

Herbaceous perennial to 2 ft. tall with square stems arising from rhizomes. Leaves 1–2 in. long, opposite narrow, glabrous and giving rise in their axes to small short branches. Flowers in numerous dense heads each about ¼ in. in diameter. Corolla pinkish, irregular and about ¼ in. long. Seeds very small. Faintly aromatic.

Dry fields, borders, Coastal Plain. Summer. Maine to South Carolina.

P. tenuifolium Schrader has very narrow leaves and is more common in the Piedmont and mountains.

109

MOUNTAIN MINT: *Pycnanthemum incanum* (Linnaeus) Michaux.

Perennial herb with square stems about 3 ft. tall. Leaves to 3 in. long, opposite, ovate, toothed and whitened beneath with very fine pubescence. Upper leaves usually conspicuously whitened on upper surfaces also. Flowers in heads up to 1 in. in diameter. Calyx lobes short. Corolla pink to rose with darker spotted lower lip. Nutlets dark. Pleasantly minty.

Woods and borders, mostly in the mountains. Summer. Virginia to South Carolina.

SKULLCAP: *Scutellaria serrata* Andrzejowski.

A square-stemmed perennial herb with opposite, ovate, toothed leaves and purple flowers borne terminally. As in the other species of this genus the calyx is 2-lipped with a protruberance on the upper.

Woods and margins. Piedmont and mountains. Spring. New Jersey to South Carolina.

S. elliptica Muhlenberg has a pubescent stem and is more common and widespread.

S. integrifolia Linnaeus has lanceolate leaves and occurs throughout from New England to Florida.

SILVERLEAF NETTLE: *Solanum elaeagnifolium* Cavanilles.

Prickly perennial herb covered with a more-or-less silvery pubescence throughout. Leaves narrowly oblong, wavy-margined and from 2–4 in. long. Flowers about 1 in. across, violet and 5-lobed. Stamens yellow and conspicuous. Fruit a yellowish berry ½ in. in diameter. Introduced from the southwestern United States. Dry roadsides and waste places. Summer. Occurs sporadically in the southeastern states.

TREAD-SOFTLY, HORSE NETTLE: *S. carolinense* Linnaeus. A native species ranging from New York to Florida. Leaf margins coarsely wavy. Flowers blue. Common in fields and waste places.

PURPLE GERARDIA, AUTUMN BELLS: *Agalinis purpurea* (Linnaeus) Pennell.

Slender-stemmed, branching annual up to 3 ft. high. Leaves opposite, very narrow and 1–2 in. long. Flowers pink to purple, spreading and with five slightly irregular lobes. Calyx very short and bell-shaped; stamens 4. Fruit a small many-seeded capsule.

Moist margins and openings. Summer and fall. New England to Florida.

Two or three other species are very similar.

STICKY FOXGLOVE: *Aureolaria pectinata* (Nuttall) Pennell.

Freely branching annual to 3 ft. tall, copiously covered with a glandular pubescence making the plant sticky to the touch. Leaves ovate in outline and much divided. Flowers 1–1½ in. long, yellow and showy. Petals 5. Capsule almost ½ in. long.

Dry, open woods of the Coastal Plain. Summer. North Carolina to Florida.

YELLOW FOXGLOVE: *A. virginica* (Linnaeus) Pennell.

Perennial to 3 ft. tall with variously shaped and lobed leaves and 1½ in. long yellow flowers. Plants little branched.

Woodlands throughout where it is perhaps associated with white oaks.

INDIAN PAINT BRUSH: *Castilleja coccinea* (Linnaeus) Sprengel.

Plant arises from a cluster of rosette leaves that are oblong and mostly entire; those of the stem are deeply and irregularly lobed. The yellow flowers are not nearly as showy as the scarlet to crimson leaves just beneath.

Meadows and margins, mountains and Piedmont. Spring and summer. New Hampshire to Florida.

This plant is somewhat root parasitic, possibly on grasses.

WHITE TURTLEHEAD: *Chelone glabra* Linnaeus.

Erect perennial to 2 ft. tall. Several stems arising from single root system. Leaves up to 5 in. long, about one-fourth as broad and sharply toothed. Flowers in dense terminal spike. Corolla 1–1½ in. long, white or tinged with color, two-lipped with upper petals arching over so as to mostly close the throat and create the fancied resemblance to a turtle's head. Fruit a capsule.

Muddy stream banks and wet woods. Summer and fall. Nova Scotia to Georgia.

C. obliqua Linnaeus has purple flowers and occurs infrequently.

MONKEY FLOWER: *Mimulus ringens* Linnaeus.

Square-stemmed perennial up to 2 ft. high from stolon forming rootstock. Leaves 2–3 in. long, half as broad, reduced upward, opposite and obscurely toothed. Flowers solitary, stalked and borne in the axils of the upper leaves. Corolla about 1 in. across, blue and with a closed throat. Capsule longer than broad and many seeded.

Swamps and pond margins. Summer. Nova Scotia to Georgia.

M. alatus Aiton differs in having leaves with petioles and a winged stem.

MULLEIN, FLANNEL PLANT: *Verbascum thapsus* Linnaeus.

Stout, densely woolly, erect biennial up to 7 ft. tall. Leaves up to 1 ft. long, as first forming a large but compact rosette but later borne progressively reduced on the tall stem. Flowers ¾ in. across, yellow and arranged in a dense spike at the top of the stem. Petals 5. Fruit a capsule. Native of Europe and widely spread in the United States.

Dry banks, roadsides and waste places. Summer.

MOTH MULLEIN: *V. blattaria* Linnaeus.

A nonwoolly species. Leaves are toothed, vary much in shape and have little or no pubescence. The 1 in. wide, 5-lobed, yellow or rarely white flowers are produced abundantly and over a long period. Capsules are ¼ in. wide and many seeded.

Native of Eurasia but occurs widely in the United States. Late spring and Summer.

BURDOCK: *Arctium minus* (Hill) Bernhardi.

A coarse biennial composite and Eurasian introduction to 3 ft. high. Leaves large, long heart-shaped, except upper, woolly beneath and commonly entire. Individual flower slender, purple and in ½ in. wide heads surrounded by incurved hooks. Weedy.

Waste places, pastures and roadsides, Piedmont and mountains. Summer. Newfoundland, south and west.

Elytraria carolinensis (J. F. Gmelin) Persoon is a basal leaved perennial from slender rhizomes. Leaves in rosette, to 7 in. long, rounded at tip, narrowed to base and entire or wavey margined. Flower stalk to 18 in. high and covered with small, closely adhering, bracteal leaves. Flowers white or blue, funnelform, somewhat 2-lipped and ⅓ in. long. Fruit a capsule.

Swamp forests, rare. Summer. Charleston south into Georgia.

CROSS-VINE: *Bignonia capreolata* Linnaeus.

Woody vine high-climbing by rootlets along the stem. Leaves consisting of two leaflets with heart-shaped bases and a tendril arising between them. Flowers leathery, 1½–2 in. long, open and bordered with 5 spreading petals. The outside part of the flower is deep orange and the inner petal surfaces are yellow. A stem section when viewed from the end reveals that the normal growth pattern forms a cross in the wood, hence the common name. Popular with Humming Birds.

Low woods and swamps. Spring. Maryland to Florida.

TRUMPET VINE, COWITCH: *Campsis radicans* (Linnaeus) Seemann.

Trumpet-shaped orange flowers and opposite leaves with 7–15 leaflets. Many habitats. Summer. New Jersey to Florida.

WILD JASMINE: *Trachelospermum difforme* (Walter) Gray.

Slender, woody, seimevergreen twining vine with brownish stems and opposite entire leaves varying from long linear to almost circular and with milky juice. Flowers small, yellow and in axillary clusters of several. Pods are very slender, paired and to 5 in. long.

Low margins and banks, lower Piedmont and Coastal plain. Early summer. Delaware to Florida and Texas.

INDIAN CIGAR, CATAWBA: *Catalpa bignonioides* Walter.

Medium sized tree with leaves 5–10 in. long, heart-shaped with pointed ends, or sometimes heart-shaped only at the base and 3-lobed beyond the middle. Flower clusters at tips of branches. Corolla 1 in. or more broad, white and spotted with purple, sometimes striped with purple or orange. Petals 5 and spreading. Fruit cigar-shaped 6–12 in; sometimes smoked by children. Seed winged. Cultivated by fishermen for caterpillars which feed on the leaves.

A variable species perhaps hybridized with forms from the Southwest and from Asia. Summer. Native of Georgia and Florida but introduced northward to New York.

PRINCESS TREE: *Paulownia tomentosa* (Thunberg) Steudel.

Similarly shaped leaves and flowers. The flowers however are light purple and appear before the leaves. The fruit is a large, short woody capsule.

Introduced from China and widely escaped.

CANCER ROOT, SQUAWROOT: *Conopholis americana* (Linnaeus) Wallroth.

A clumped, short, stout nongreen root parasite, probably on oaks. Numerous pale flowers are followed by many-seeded capsules.

Dry woods. Spring. Nova Scotia to Florida and west.

BUTTERWORT: *Pinguicula caerulea* Walter.

Perennial herb forming a rosette of leaves at ground level. Leaves 1–2 in. long and enrolled from the sides; surface somewhat sticky. The enrolling habit is thought to have beneficial value in that small insects are trapped and their disintegrating bodies provide mineral nutrients that are absorbed by the leaf. Flowers raised 4–6 in. on leafless stalk, pale violet and about ¾ in. wide. Corolla of 5 notched petals and a spur. Fruit a capsule.

Low, open woods, Coastal Plain. Spring. North Carolina to Florida.

P. lutea Walter is less common, has yellow flowers and ranges the lower Coastal Plain from mid North Carolina to Florida.

RUELLIA : *Ruellia carolinensis* (Walter) Steudel.

Erect pubescent perennial to 18 in. high with ovate leaves to 2 in. long. Flowers from the axils, blue and Petunialike. Fruit a capsule.

Dry woods, throughout. Summer. New Jersey to Florida.

Dicliptera brachiata (Pursh) Sprengel is a perennial herb to 30 in. tall with opposite, ovate, petioled leaves to 4 in. long. Flowers in axillary clusters subtended by small green bracts. Corolla pink or bluish, funnelform and 2 lipped. Capsule flattened.

Low woods, lower Piedmont and Coastal Plain. Summer. Virginia to Florida.

Justicia americana (Linnaeus) Vahl is a plant to 2 ft. tall from coarse rhizomes. Leaves opposite, narrow and to 6 in. long. Flowers violet and raised on slender stalk from leaf axils. Capsules flattened and mostly 4-seeded.

Sandy or rocky steam beds, lower Piedmont and Coastal Plain. Summer. Quebec to Georgia.

117

BLADDERWORT: *Utricularia inflata* Walter.

Small aquatic herb with submerged stems and leaves with capillary divisions bearing tiny bladders which trap microscopic animal forms whose decaying bodies presumably supply a form of foliar fertilizer to the plant. At flowering time 5–10 curious, inflated branch stems develop at the tip of the main stem and, serving as floats, lift it to the surface where an emergent flowering stem 6–10 in. tall develops. Flowers ¾ in. wide, yellow and two-lipped. Fruit a small capsule.

Quiet ponds and ditches. Spring and summer. New Jersey to Florida.

Several species lacking inflated leaves are common in the Coastal Plain. Most have yellow flowers but one has purple and one has white.

BUTTON BUSH: *Cephalanthus occidentalis* Linnaeus.

Deciduous shrub usually less than 7 ft. tall. Leaves opposite or in whorls of three, 2½–5 in. long and half as wide with smooth margins. Flowers small and numerous in densely packed, spherical heads about 1 in. in diameter. Styles elongated much past the petals. Seeds small.

Swamp and stream margins. Summer. Nova Scotia to Florida.

BLUET: *Houstonia caerulea* Linnaeus.

Delicate perennial with erect stems up to 5 in. high. Leaves very small and mostly in a basal rosette, those of the stem opposite. Flowers usually less than ½ in. in diameter and raised above the leaves. Corolla of 4 widely spreading petals, blue with a yellow eye. Fruit a several-seeded capsule.

Stream margins, fields and clearings. Spring. Nova Scotia to Georgia.

H. patens Elliott is a similar but somewhat smaller-flowered species lacking a yellow eye in the deep blue corolla.

Habitat and flowering time as above. Virginia to Florida.

H. purpurea Linnaeus is a very variable species. Perennial from winter rosette, gone by flowering time. Leaves sessile, lanceolate to ovate and to 2 in. long. Flowers deep lavender to white, about ¼ in. long and pubescent within.

Forests, roadsides and clearings. Summer. New Jersey to Alabama.

PARTRIDGE BERRY: *Mitchella repens* Linnaeus.

A small prostrate evergreen with opposite, ovate, leathery leaves to ½ in. long. Flowers axillary, white or pinkish and in pairs. Berry red.

Rich, moist woods, throughout. Spring. Newfoundland to Florida.

BUTTONWEED: *Diodia virginiana* Linnaeus.

Perennial with lanceolate leaves to 2 in. long and white flowers with 4 spreading lobes, pubescent on the inside. Fruit ¼ in. long, pubescent ribbed and splitting into 2, indehiscent, 1-seeded parts.

Wet, open ground, throughout. Summer and fall. New Jersey to Florida.

D. teres Walter is an annual; a smaller, more erect plant with narrow leaves to 1 in. long and small pinkish or white flowers. Fruit about ⅛ in. long, not ribbed, otherwise as above.

Sandy fields, margins and roadsides, throughout. Summer and fall. New England to the Gulf of Mexico.

FEVER TREE: *Pinckneya pubens* Michaux.

Deciduous shrub or occasionally small tree. Leaves oval, 2–5 in. long, pubescent and with smooth margins. Flowers about ¾ in. long, in small clusters, greenish with brownish markings. Petals 5 and recurved. Sepals 5 and short except for one which is conspicuously enlarged to about half leaf size and is white or pinkish-white. Fruit a ½ in. long capsule.

Swamp margins, Coastal Plain. Spring and summer. South Carolina to Florida.

Manettia glabra Chamisso and Schlectendahl. Glabrous, semievergreen, twining plant with opposite, lanceolate, petioled leaves and tubular red flowers that are yellow within and have 5 short, reflexed lobes.

Introduced from South America as an ornamental and sometimes persists long after cultivation.

WOODBINE, TRUMPET HONEYSUCKLE: *Lonicera sempervirens* Linnaeus.

Semievergreen, woody twiner climbing to a height of only a few feet. Leaves opposite, 1½–3 in. long and thickish. The upper 2 or 3 pairs of leaves on a branch are often joined together so as to make the stem appear to pass through the middle of a leaf. Flowers trumpet-shaped, deep red. Petals 5. Fruit a red berry.

Woods and margins. Spring and summer. New England to Florida.

YELLOW HONEYSUCKLE: *Lonicera flava* Sims.

Low-climbing woody vine with opposite entire leaves, the upper ones commonly grown together at base. Flowers are yellow.

Wooded borders and rocky ledges, mountains. Summer. North Carolina to Georgia and west.

JAPANESE HONEYSUCKLE: *L. japonica* Thunberg.

Introduced from Asia and is now naturalized from New England to Florida and very pernicious. Flowers are white the first day, yellow the second.

ELDERBERRY: *Sambucus canadensis* Linnaeus.

Deciduous shrub usually less than 8 ft. tall with weak, gray stems containing a very large core of pith. Leaves opposite, each with 5–11 sharply serrated leaflets. Flowers small, white, fragrant and in heavy terminal clusters. Petals usually 5. Fruit a small red or black edible berry.

Roadsides and stream margins. Summer. New England to Georgia.

S. pubens Michaux is similar but has a paniculate rather than a flat-topped inflorscence and red berries instead of black.

Moist openings at high elevations. Late spring. Newfoundland to North Carolina.

MAPLE-LEAVED VIBURNUM, DOCKMACKIE: *Viburnum acerifolium* Linnaeus.

Deciduous shrub seldom over 3 ft. tall. Leaves 2–4 in. long, 3-lobed and shallowly toothed, opposite and unusually colorful in Autumn. Flowers creamy, small, in showy flat-topped clusters raised well above the leaves. Fruit fleshy, 1-seeded and black when ripe.

Woods and bluffs inland. Spring. New Brunswick to Florida.

ARROW-WOOD: *Viburnum dentatum* Linnaeus.

Deciduous shrub usually less than 7 ft. high. Leaves broadly elliptic, opposite, with prominent straight veins and distinct teeth. Flowers small and in heavy clusters at the tips of the slender branches. Petals usually 5. Fruit fleshy, 1-seeded and bluish-black.

Moist woods and borders. Summer. New England to Florida.

BLACK HAW: *V. prunifolium* Linnaeus.

A large shrub or small tree with closely checkered bark and opposite, elliptic, finely serrated leaves 1–2 in. long. New England to Florida. Three or more other species also occur.

CARDINAL FLOWER: *Lobelia cardinalis* Linnaeus.

Erect, usually unbranched perennial herb. Leaves up to 4 in. long and a third as broad, alternate and irregularly toothed. Flowers in terminal racemens and strikingly conspicuous. Corolla cardinal red, 1–1½ in. long and with 5 lobes arranged two above and three below. Fruit a many-seeded capsule.

Wet open places. Late summer. New Brunswick to Florida.

Several other species occur, all of which are blue or white flowered. Some are small and very delicate. The largest flowered blue is *L. siphilitica* Linnaeus and is confined to wet mountain meadows. Other blues are *L. puberula* Michaux with a downy stem and widespread and *L. elongata* Small with a smooth stem and common on the Coastal Plain.

WINGSTEM: *Actinomeris alternifolia* (Linnaeus) De Candolle.

A tall perennial with alternate leaves, or the lower oppposite. A thin winglike green membrane extends from the base of one leaf to that of the one below, etc. Flowers are yellow, the rays usually drooping while the crown is a globular disk of tiny tubular flowers.

Low woods and margins, mountains and Piedmont. Summer. New York to Florida and west.

Several other plants have winged stems and are so named.

LARGE-FLOWERED ASTER: *Aster paludosus* Aiton.

Perennial from well developed rhizomes. Stems rather weak and up to 2½ ft. tall. Leaves narrow, obscurely veined except for the midrib, not toothed, 10 to 20 times longer than wide and pointing closely up the stem. Heads few to several, 1½ in. across, or even larger. Rays 20–40 and pinkish-violet. Disk yellow. This is one of the largest and handsomest asters.

Open, moist sandy ground. Coastal Plain. Fall. North Carolina to Florida.

WHITE-TOPPED ASTER, FROST FLOWER: *Aster pilosus* Willdenow.

Erect, branching perennial up to 4½ ft. tall, basal and lower stem leaves soon lost. Middle and upper stem leaves sessile, narrowly elliptic, barely toothed or entire, up to 3 in. long and smooth or hairy. Heads usually numerous ½–¾ in. wide. Rays white; disk yellow. A variable species.

Moist borders and open places. Fall. Maine to Georgia.

WHITE-TOPPED ASTER: *Aster reticulatus* (Pursh) Greene.

Perennial up to 2 ft. tall from strong rootstock. Leaves elliptic to obovate, entire and to 3 in. long. Heads about 1 in. broad and borne in open terminal clusters. Rays white, or whitish, and very slender. Disk yellow.

Low woods of the Coastal Plain. Spring. South Carolina to Florida.

WALTER'S ASTER: *Aster squarrosus* Walter.

Perennial with spreading, loosely branched stems. Leaves of two types. The basal oblanceolate, 2–3 in. long and with rounded tips; those of the stem ovate, fleshly, stiffly spreading and only about ¼ in. long. Heads scattered, each about ¾ in. wide. Rays pale purple. Disk yellow.

Dry woodlands of the Coastal Plain. Fall. North Carolina to Florida.

LEOPARD'S-BANE: *Arnica acaulis* (Walter) Britton, Sterns and Poggenberg.

Perennial to 2 ft. tall from short, thick rootstock. Leaves mostly basal, 2–4 in. long, broadly elliptic, obscurely toothed and coarsely hairy. Stem leaves few; lower opposite, upper alternate. Heads several and up to 2½ in. wide. Rays 12–20 and yellow. Disk yellow, many-flowered and depressed in center. It was formerly sought by herb collectors for its reputed medicinal value.

Low pinelands and clearings. Summer. Delaware to Florida.

GREEN-EYES: *Berlandiera pumila* (Michaux) Nuttall.

Thick-rooted perennial has alternate, rather coarsely toothed, leaves that are rough hairy on both sides. The center flowers at first are green but become yellowish. The bright yellow ray flowers produce blackish achenes.

Sandy margins, woods and old fields, lower Piedmont and upper Coastal Plain. Late spring until frost. South Carolina to Florida.

Photo by Mike Creel

126

SAND THISTLE: *Carduus repandus* (Michaux) Persoon.

Deep rooted perennial to 2 ft. tall. Leaves numerous, narrow, to 6 in. long, irregularly toothed or lobed and spiny on the margins. Heads few, 1–1½ in. high, subtended by many involucral bracts each tipped with a slender but weak spine. Corollas pinkish-purple. Achenes small and bearing a tuft of capillary bristles.

Open ground in the Coastal Plain. Summer. Virginia to Florida.

HORRIBLE THISTLE: *C. spinosissimus* Walter.

A stout biennial with a stem to 1½ in. in diameter and covered with a cottony pubescence; Leaves to 1 ft. long, much dissected and spiny; flowers purplish-red, or sometimes yellow.

Roadsides, pastures and waste areas, Piedmont and Coastal Plain. Spring. Maine to Florida.

CARPEPHORUS: *Carpephorus bellidifolius* (Michaux) Torrey and Gray.

Low, fibrous-rooted perennial herb. Leaves mostly basal, alternate, lanceolate on slender petioles, glabrous and not toothed. Flowering stems 6–12 in. high and branched. Flower heads rose-purple and many-flowered.

Dry, sandy woods of the Coastal Plain. Late summer and fall. Virginia to Florida.

BACHELOR'S-BUTTON: *Centaurea cyanus* Linnaeus.

Rather stout branching annual to 3 ft. tall. Leaves and stem whitened with appressed pubescence. Leaves linear, up to 4 in. long, and lower sometimes toothed. Heads about 1½ in. in diameter, blue, purple, pink or white. Ray flowers absent, disk flowers enlarged and irregularly lobed. Introduced from the Mediterranean region, widely cultivated for ornament and widely established as a weed along roadsides and in waste places. Summer and fall.

CHICORY: *Cichorium intybus* Linnaeus.

A roadside plant making a rather similar appearance. It differs mainly in having only ray flowers, no little ones in the center.

WHITE DAISY, OXEYE DAISY: *Chrysanthemum leucanthemum* Linnaeus.

Clump-forming perennial with stems to 2 ft. high. Leaves narrow, coarsely and irregularly toothed; the lower petioled and widest above the middle, the upper sessile. Heads to 2 in. across and mostly raised above the leaves on slender stalks. Rays 20–25 and white. Disk flattened, many flowered and yellow.

Late summer and fall.

A widely introduced European species.

GREEN AND GOLD: *Chrysogonum virginianum* Linnaeus.

Horizontally spreading, hairy perennial. Leaves opposite, ovate, peti-oled and shallowly toothed. Flower heads about 1 in. across. Rays and disk yellow. Rays usually 5 and relatively broad. This is one of the very earliest spring flowers.

Moist deciduous woods. Early spring. Pennsylvania to Florida.

Available now as a cultivar.

COTTONY GOLDEN ASTER: *Chrysopsis gossypina* (Michaux) Elliott.

Low perennial characterized by all-over cottonyness or cobwebbyness. Leaves 1–2½ in. long and with smooth margins. Flower heads few, about 1½ in. across when fully open. Ray flowers about 20; rays and disk yellow.

Dry sterile sites, Coastal Plain. Late summer and fall. Virginia to Florida.

C. mariana (Linnaeus) Elliott is pubescent but not cottony, has some-what smaller heads and occurs throughout. Late summer and fall. New York to Florida.

GRASS-LEAVED GOLDEN ASTER: *Chrysopsis graminifolia* (Michaux) Elliott.

Slender perennial with closely appressed silvery pubescence throughout. Leaves 4–10 in. long, parallel-veined and grasslike but somewhat broader in the middle than at the base. Stem leaves much reduced. Flowering stem with spreading branches. Flower heads about ¾ in. across. Ray and disk flowers yellow. Rays 12–15.

Dry woods and openings. Summer. Virginia to Florida.

SHRUBBY GOLDENROD: *Chrysoma pauciflosculosa* (Michaux) Greene.

Shrubby evergreen up to 3 ft. tall. Leaves alternate, leathery with roughened surfaces, narrow and crowded toward the tips of the stems. Flowers raised well above the leaves. Heads numerous, few-flowered and yellow. Branches of the inflorescence also yellow. A rare plant with very local distribution.

Sandy woods and coastal sands. Fall. South Carolina to Florida.

RAYLESS GOLDENROD: *Chondrophora nudata* (Michaux) Britton.

Glabrous or somewhat viscid perennial from basal rosette of narrow long-stemmed leaves. Flowering stem to 2 ft. tall and with a few small alternate leaves.   The flat-topped inflorescence is made up of many few-flowered heads. Flowers, bracts around the head and supporting banches all yellow.

Bays and savannahs, Coastal Plain. Late summer. North Carolina to Florida.

Chrysoma pauciflosculosa

COREOPSIS: *Coreopsis lanceolata* Linnaeus.

Perennial to 2 ft. high from short, stout rootstock. Leaves very narrowly lanceolate with 2–4 lateral lobes sometimes present, hairy and not toothed on margin. The lower leaves are long petioled; the upper almost sessile. Heads about 2 in. in diameter. Rays wide and 5-toothed at tip. Rays and disk yellow. Showy.

Roadsides, waste places and borders. Summer. Delaware to Florida.

C. major Walter is also widely distributed. Perennial with opposite sessile leaves, each deeply divided into 3 lanceolate or linear nearly separate segments, giving the appearance of 6 leaves in a whorl. Heads 1½ in. wide, yellow with yellow or darker center.

C. tinctoria Nuttall is an annual introduced from farther west as an ornamental. Leaves, at least the lower, opposite and divided into narrow segments. Heads numerous; rays yellow with reddish-brown bases.

Moist roadsides, fields and margins, mostly throughout. Spring and summer. Minnesota to Louisiana and west.

SILVERLING, GROUNDSEL, SEA-MYRTLE: *Baccharis halimifolia* Linnaeus.

A nearly evergreen shrub to 10 ft. high with grayish to dull green leaves to 3 in. long, coarsely toothed toward tips. A single plant produces only staminate or only pistillate flowers, all rayless and grouped into small heads. At maturity the cluster of small achenes in each head develop silky bristles that extend and make a conspicuous appearance, hense the name Silverling.

More common along the coast but widespread inland. Summer and fall. Massachusetts to Florida.

DOG FENNEL: *Eupatorium compositifolium* Walter.

Erect, clump-forming perennial to 5 ft. tall. Leaves 2–3 in. long but much divided into linear segments. Flowers very small and borne 3–6 together in small heads. The flower-bearing portion of the plant is terminal and plumelike. Corolla too small for observation without a hand lens.

Abandoned fields and dry open woods mostly in the Coastal Plain. Summer and fall. North Carolina to Florida.

E. capillifolium (Lamarck) Small is a similar species but with leaf segments that are threadlike.

New Jersey to Florida.

JOE-PYE WEED: *Eupatorium purpureum* Linnaeus.

Erect, nonclump-forming perennial attaining a height to 7 ft. Stem hollow and sometimes used for drinking straws by outdoorsmen. Leaves in whorls of 3 or more, 4–8 in. long, lanceolate and sharply toothed. Flowers creamy-pink, very small and borne 3–7 together in slender heads. Flowering portion terminal and with rounded top.

Stream banks and low, open woods in the mountains. Summer. New Hampshire to Florida.

E. dubium Willdenow is similar but has broader, shorter leaves that are 3-nerved at the base, purple-speckled stem, darker flowers and occurs mostly in the Coastal Plain. Nova Scotia to South Carolina.

BLANKETFLOWER: *Gaillardia pulchella* Fougeroux.

Low, freely branched annual seldom over a foot high. Leaves narrow, blunt at the tips, usually not toothed and somewhat whitened on the upper surface by long hairs. Heads about 1½ in. wide. Rays 8–12, 3-lobed and purple with yellow tips. Disk brown and many flowered.

Coastal sandy wastes and inland. Summer. Virginia to Florida. Originally limited to Florida and westward. Now being used as an ornamental.

SNEEZEWEED: *Helenium flexuosum* Rafinesque.

Erect branching perennial up to 2½ ft. high from fibrous root system. Stem winged downward from the leaf bases. Leaves 1–4 in. long, alternate, narrow and pointed up the stem. Flower heads showy, about 1½ in. in diameter. Rays 6–12, yellow and 3-lobed. Disk brown or purplish-brown, many-flowered and globose in shape.

Stream banks and moist open places. Late summer and fall. North Carolina to Georgia but widely spread as a weed.

BITTERWEED: *H. amarum* (Rafinesque) H. Rock.

Similar but smaller flowers; numerous, narrowly linear leaves and grows as a common weed along roadsides, in overgrazed pastures and in waste places.

Late spring to fall. Virginia to Florida.

Helenium flexuosum

SUNFLOWER: *Helianthus decapetalus* Linnaeus.

Erect perennials to 4 ft. high with well developed rhizomes. Leaves opposite, ovate, pointed, 3-nerved, toothed and short petioled. Flower heads to 3 in. wide and appearing conspicuously large. Ray flowers 10–20 and yellow. Disk flowers yellow.

Bottom lands and stream banks in the mountains and Piedmont. Late summer. Maine to South Carolina.

H. divaricatus Linnaeus has sessile leaves, smaller flowers and is found in drier habitats throughout.

H. microcephalus Torrey and Gray is similar to *H. divaricatus* but has petioled leaves. Throughout.

TALL SUNFLOWER: *Helianthus giganteus* Linnaeus.

Usually erect, little-branched perennial up to 8 ft. high from rhizome-bearing rootstock. Leaves alternate, pubescent, lanceolate, toothed, short petioled and to 6 in. long. Flower heads to 3 in. wide. Rays 10–20 and yellow. Disk yellowish-brown.

Wet borders, stream banks, etc. Late summer. South Carolina and north.

OXEYE: *Heliopsis helianthoides* (Linnaeus) Britton, Sterns and Poggenburg.

Perennial to 4 ft. high from short rhizome. Leaves opposite, broadly lanceolate, toothed, to 6 in. long and abruptly petioled. Heads several, terminal and showy. Rays and center yellow. Rays 1½ in. long.

Woods and meadows, mountains and Piedmont. Summer. Canada to Georgia.

Helianthus giganteus

CAMPHORWEED: *Heterotheca subaxillaris* (Lamarck) Britton and Rusby.

A very variable species. Biennial or annual, erect or widely branched and to 3½ ft. tall. Leaves alternate, rough to the touch, variously toothed or entire, the lower with petioles, the upper sessile and clasping the stem. Flower heads numerous and from ½–1¼ in. wide. Ray and disk flowers yellow. This plant was introduced from areas farther south and west.

It is now well established and is perhaps the most conspicuous weedy species in abandoned fields and waste places in the late summer and fall. Delaware to Florida.

GRASS-LEAVED BLAZING STAR: *Liatris graminifolia* Willdenow.

Stem or stems to 3 ft. high arising from globose rootstock. Leaves numerous, linear and to 5 in. long; the upper shorter. Heads numerous forming a spikelike inflorescence. Subtending bracts and flowers purple.

Open woods and old fields throughout. Fall. New Jersey to Florida and Alabama.

L. squarrosa (Linnaeus) Michaux may be recognized by the large recurved bracts surrounding the flowers.

BARBARA'S BUTTONS: *Marshallia trinervia* (Walter) Trelease.

Glabrous perennial up to 2 ft. tall from rhizome-forming base. Leaves narrow, up to 4 in. long, 3-nerved and smooth-margined. Lower leaves petioled, upper sessile. Heads solitary on long stalks, 2 in. in diameter and pink. Ray flowers absent.

Moist pinelands and clearings in the Coastal Plain. Late spring. Virginia to Florida.

M. obovata (Walter) Beadle & Boynton has thicker, blunter leaves, white or pinkish flowers and is more widespread.

MARSH FLEABANE, CAMPHOR WEED: *Pluchea camphorata* (Linnaeus) De Candolle.

Perennial from fibrous root system sending up usually two or more upright stems. Leaves alternate, finely toothed, to 4 in. long and strong scented. Flower heads small, pinkish or purplish and in clusters arising from the axils of the upper leaves.

Wet margins, ditches and shores. Summer. Delaware to Florida.

TETRAGONOTHECA: *T. helianthoides* Linnaeus.

Perennial to 3 ft. tall with 1–several stems from root crown. Leaves opposite, elliptic or wider, narrowed to base but sessile and coarsely toothed. Head terminal, solitary and surrounded by 4 green ovate bracts 1 in. long each. Rays yellow, toothed at tip and 1 in. or more long.

Sandy woods and margins, Piedmont and upper Coastal Plain. Early summer. Virginia to Florida.

136

PINK MARSH FLEABANE: *Pluchea rosea* Godfrey.

Pubescent perennial to 3 ft. tall with alternate, oblong, sessile leaves with clasping bases. Heads many flowered and in compact gloms. Corollas filiform, tubular and pink.

Low woods, savannahs and ditches, Coastal Plain. Late summer. North Carolina to Florida.

P. foetida (Linnaeus) De Candolle is quite similar but has creamy white corollas.

Habitat and flowering time as above. New Jersey to Florida and west.

BEAR'S-FOOT: *Polymnia uvedalia* Linnaeus.

Stout, branched perennial reaching a height of 8 ft. Leaves alternate, large, and coarsely and irregularly toothed. Flower heads about 1½ in. wide. Ray and disk flowers yellow. Rays about 8. Achenes few, large, more or less globular and black and produced only by ray flowers.

Moist borders and stream banks. Fall. New York to Florida.

RAGWORT, BITTERWEED:
Senecio smallii Britton.

Clump-forming perennial with deeply and sometimes finely lobed leaves and usually a somewhat woolly stem. A weedy species.

Roadsides, pastures and margins. May and June. New Jersey to Florida.

S. glabellus Poiret is an annual preferring swamp forests and other low places. Spring. Coastal Plain and Piedmont of South Carolina then south into Florida.

S. aureus Linnaeus has long petioled, cordate leaves. Meadows and bogs, mountains and Piedmont but barely into South Carolina. Spring. Southern Canada to Georgia.

WHITE-TOPPED ASTER: *Sericocarpus linifolius* (Linnaeus) Britton, Sterns and Poggenberg.

Perennial to 2 ft. high. Leaves narrow, rather numerous, to 3 in. long and smooth margined. Flower heads ¾–1 in. wide. Rays about 5. Ray and disk flowers white.

Dry woods and clearings. Summer. New England to Georgia.

S. asteroides (Linnaeus) Britton, Sterns and Poggenberg is similar but with broader, toothed leaves.

Balduina uniflora Nuttall is an erect, little-branched perennial to 2 ft. tall. Leaves alternate, entire, widely elliptic, with narrow bases and to 2 in. long. Flower head surrounded by 3–5 rows of green bracts. Ray and disk flowers yellow. Rays 1 in. long and 3-toothed at tip.

Savannahs and bays, Coastal Plain. Late summer. North Carolina to Florida.

TALL GOLDENROD: *Solidago altissima* Linnaeus.

Perennial herb from strong fibrous roots and rhizomes. Leaves alternate, 3-nerved, rough pubescent above, narrowly elliptic and usually shallowly toothed. Lower leaves dead or missing at flowering time. Inflorescence pointed at the top. Heads small, numerous, several-flowered and yellow. State flower of Kentucky.

Roadsides, field margins and thin woods. Fall. Quebec to Florida.

Numerous other species occur. One of the easiest to recognize is *S. odora* Aiton. Found in open woods, savannahs and dry margins, it has entire, lanceolate leaves with rounded bases that when held up to the light show the presence of many tiny translucent dots. When crushed leaves give off the fragrance of anise. The dried leaves have been used for a pleasant tea.

It occurs throughout. Late summer and fall. Massachusetts to Florida.

TINY-HEADED GOLDENROD: *Solidago microcephala* (Greene) Bush.

Bushy-topped perennial 1½–3 ft. tall and glabrous or nearly so throughout. Leaves very narrow, up to 3 in. long but progressively much shorter upward. Lower portion of the stem becoming leafless at flowering time. Flower heads small, numerous and yellow.

Dry open woods, fields and roadsides; lower Piedmont and Coastal Plain. Late summer. New Jersey to Florida.

139

HOUND'S-TONGUE: *Trilisa paniculata* (Walter) Cassini.

Erect perennial to 3½ ft. high from short rootstock. Stem sticky pubescent. Leaves mostly basal, up to 6 in. long, elliptic, rather thick and sometimes slightly toothed. Stem leaves progressively much smaller and narrower upward. Flower heads rose-purple and forming a conspicuous terminal inflorescence. Ray flowers absent. Disk flowers several in each of the slender heads. Branches and bracts of the inflorescence also purple.

Low open woods of the Coastal Plain. Fall. North Carolina to Florida.

DEER'S-TONGUE OR VANILLA PLANT: *T. odoratissima* (Walter) Cassini.

Plant has a smooth stem and is very fragrant because of the coumarin in the leaves. Once used to add aroma and flavor to tobacco.

QUININE WEED: *Parthenium intergrifolium* Linnaeus.

A perennial herb to 3 ft. tall from thickened roots. Leaves mostly basal, to 6 in. long and with long petioles; stem leaves often sessile. Flowers white and in heads ½ in. wide. Rays 3–5 and so short as to be barely seen. Archenes dark and flattened.

Dry woods and margins, Piedmont and mountains. Summer. Maryland to Georgia.

AGERATUM, MIST FLOWER: *Eupatorium coelestinum* Linnaeus.

Erect perennial to 2 ft. high from rhizomes. Leaves are opposite, ovate, long-pointed, to 3 in. long and toothed. Flowers are in small heads, all rayless and violet to bluish.

Moist margins and open areas, mostly Coastal Plain. Summer. New Jersey to Florida.

Most other *Eupatoria* in the Carolinas have white flowers.

YELLOW WINGSTEM: *Verbesina occidentalis* (Linnaeus) Walter.

Coarse, erect perennial to 6 ft. high. Stems with 4 green membranous wings extending downward from the leaf bases. Leaves opposite, ovate, toothed and up to 6 in. long. Flower heads terminal and rather small. Ray flowers few and yellow. Disk flowers yellow.

Rich moist thickets. Late summer and fall. Maryland to Florida.

V. virginica Linnaeus is similar but has alternate leaves, white flowers, less conspicuous wings and is less common.

IRONWEED: *Vernonia acaulis* (Walter) Gleason.

Perennial stemless herb. Leaves 6–12 in. long, elliptic, conspicuously veined and finely toothed. Flower stalk to 30 in. high and branched toward the top. Flowers in compact heads about ¾ in. in diameter. Corollas purple and with 5 slender, spreading lobes.

Dry open woods and margins in the Coastal Plain. Summer. North Carolina to Florida.

SEA OXEYE: *Borrichia frutescens* (Linnaeus) De Candolle.

A somewhat fleshy or rubbery semievergreen shrub, forming colonies from rhizomes. Leaves opposite, entire, oblanceolate, to 3 in. long and sharp pointed. Flower heads about ½ in wide. Rays yellow and ½ in. long.

Brackish marshes and muddy beaches. Summer. Virginia to Florida.

141

IRONWEED: *Vernonia noveboracensis* (Linnaeus) Michaux.

A leafy stemmed perennial to 8 ft. tall. Leaves to 8 in. long. Heads numerous and in rather loose arrangement. Flowers tubular and purple. Bristles atop achenes purplish brown and conspicuous after flowering.

Low woods, moist openings and stream banks. Late summer. New England to Georgia.

V. glauca (Linnaeus) Willdenow differs by having pale tan bristles and leaves that are pale beneath.

Habitat, flowering time and range about the same.

RABBIT TOBACCO, EVERLASTING: *Gnaphalium obtusifolium* Linnaeus.

An erect biennial to 2 ft. high; stem matted with white, cobwebby hairs. Leaves alternate, numerous, sessile, narrow, smooth above and white cobwebby beneath. Flowers extremely slender and many crowded into narrow heads. Rays none. Plant has a rather balsamlike fragrance. Reportedly a winter food for deer and turkey.

Old fields, roadsides and open woods, throughout. Summer. Nova Scotia to Florida, Manitoba and Texas.

CUDWEED: *G. purpureum* Linnaeus.

Shorter stem, wider leaves progressively smaller toward top, purple color in the flower heads and no aroma.

Very common, throughout. Spring. United States, Mexico and South America.

INDIAN PLANTAIN: *Cacalia atriplicifolia* Linnaeus.

Glabrous perennial to 7 ft. tall with broad, palmately veined leaves that are variously lobed and toothed and very white beneath. Flower heads numerous, cylindrical and cream colored. Five cream disk flowers are in each head, none with rays.

Woods and margins, throughout. Summer. New Jersey to Georgia.

142

Index

144

145

151